T0015454

PRAISE FOR *STEADY, CALM, AND BRAVE*

"Interweaving engaging personal stories, practical Buddhist wisdom, and modern psychological insight, Kimberly Brown offers a wealth of accessible contemplative resources to address the challenges and experiences so many of us are facing in these times. The warmth and wisdom I have come to know from her presence are reflected in her words. May this collection of skillful methods for cultivating kindness and sanity be of great benefit to beings."—Dzogchen Ponlop Rinpoche, author of *Rebel Buddha* and *Emotional Rescue*

"Here is grounded, kind advice from a good spiritual friend, and my friend, Kimberly Brown. We need wise ways to think, especially now in these fraught times—because by helping ourselves, we can then help others."—Venerable Robina Courtin, Buddhist teacher

"With relatable and illuminating stories and clear, practical meditations, the offerings in *Steady, Calm, and Brave* are both timely and timeless."—Chris Grosso, author of *Indie Spiritualist* and *Dead Set on Living*

STEADY, CALM, AND BRAVE

25 Buddhist Practices of Resilience
and Wisdom in a Crisis

KIMBERLY BROWN

 Prometheus Books

Essex, Connecticut

 Prometheus Books

An imprint of Globe Pequot, the trade division of
The Rowman & Littlefield Publishing Group, Inc.
4501 Forbes Blvd., Ste. 200
Lanham, MD 20706
www.rowman.com

Distributed by NATIONAL BOOK NETWORK

British Library Cataloguing in Publication Information available

Library of Congress Cataloging-in-Publication Data Available

ISBN 978-1-63388-821-0 (pbk. : alk. paper) | ISBN 978-1-63388-822-7 (ebook)

♾️™ The paper used in this publication meets the minimum requirements of American National Standard for Information Sciences—Permanence of Paper for Printed Library Materials, ANSI/NISO Z39.48-1992.

To all my teachers, past, present, and future

I have arrived, I am home
In the here, in the now
I am solid, I am free
In the ultimate I dwell
    —THICH NHAT HAHN[1]

Contents

Preface   xi

Acknowledgments   xv

Notes on the Practices   xvii

CHAPTER 1: How Will I Get through This?   1
Practice 1: Making Room   4

CHAPTER 2: Don't Make It Worse   7
Practice 2: Coming to Your Senses   10

CHAPTER 3: Living with Uncertainty   13
Practice 3: Steady Mind   17

CHAPTER 4: Suffering Is Not a Dirty Word   19
Practice 4: Saying Yes   22

CHAPTER 5: Hope and Trust   23
Practice 5: Gladden Your Mind   27

CHAPTER 6: Love Yourself   29
Practice 6: Learning to Love   32

CHAPTER 7: Living with Grief and Loss   33
Practice 7: Finding Peace   36

CHAPTER 8: When Your Family Is Making You Crazy   39
Practice 8: I See You, Anger   43

CONTENTS

CHAPTER 9: Watching a Crisis Unfold   45
  Practice 9: Opening Your Heart to the World   48

CHAPTER 10: Just Relax   51
  Practice 10: Giving It Up to the Universe   54

CHAPTER 11: When You Need Help   57
  Practice 11: Giving and Receiving   61

CHAPTER 12: When You're Mad at the World   63
  Practice 12: Letting Your Heart Break   67

CHAPTER 13: What to Do When You're Afraid   69
  Practice 13: Facing Fear   72

CHAPTER 14: When Others Behave Badly   75
  Practice 14: Letting Go   79

CHAPTER 15: When You're Restless and Bored   81
  Practice 15: Looking Closer   85

CHAPTER 16: A Crisis of Faith   87
  Practice 16: Restoring Trust   91

CHAPTER 17: Living Alone in a Crisis   93
  Practice 17: Being Here for You   96

CHAPTER 18: Don't Lose Yourself   97
  Practice 18: Coming Home   100

CHAPTER 19: Do No Harm   101
  Practice 19: Creating Safety   104

CHAPTER 20: Navigating a Health Crisis   105
  Practice 20: May All Be Healed   109

CHAPTER 21: A Note on Thoughts and Prayers   111
  Practice 21: Effective Praying   113

CHAPTER 22: Maybe You Need a Break 115
Practice 22a: Time for Yourself 119
Practice 22b: Mindful Walking 120

CHAPTER 23: Be Joyful When You Can 123
Practice 23: Sharing Delight 126

CHAPTER 24: Don't Be Afraid to Give 129
Practice 24: Gratitude 133

CHAPTER 25: What's Next? 135
Practice 25: Awakening to Change 139

APPENDIX A: Mindfulness Meditation Instructions 141

APPENDIX B: *Metta* Meditation Instructions 143

APPENDIX C: Healing the World Meditation 145

APPENDIX D: Brahmavihara *Paritta*: Protection Chant of the Four Immeasurable Qualities 147

Notes 149

About the Author 153

Preface

After mountains, more mountains.
—Haitian proverb

I originally wrote this book in 2020, a few months after the COVID-19 pandemic began. My family, friends, students, and the world were in shock and terrified of this unimaginable crisis, and I wanted to share Buddhist tools and meditations to support everyone through it. But as we waited for the pandemic to abate and for things to "return to normal," I realized that even after it ended, there would be another crisis, because, far from being a unique situation, a crisis is a normal part of our lives, one that we will all experience many times. As we struggled through coronavirus quarantines and restrictions, other disasters, catastrophes, and tragedies continued—wildfires throughout the American Northwest, devasting floods throughout Australia, famine due to drought in Angola, and a heartbreaking military withdrawal in Afghanistan. My father's health declined and he died, my doctor learned that her acute and worsening back pain was actually Stage 4 cancer, and my cousin's wife suddenly left him without warning after nearly a decade of marriage.

The truth is, you will never be "crisis free," however much you wish to escape the unexpected, dangerous, and devastating. This might seem like bad news and maybe even the last thing you want to hear right now. But it's an inescapable fact of life that things come together and things fall apart, and it doesn't matter whether you want them to or not. Our resistance to this creates what the Buddha calls *dukkha*—unnecessary suffering, unease, or stress—that makes our human difficulties even more painful and hard. This book is a guide to understanding and recognizing your *dukkha*, offering compassion to your *dukkha*, and letting go of your *dukkha* so that you can be free to enjoy the beauty and connection we all share even in the worst circumstances and to see clearly even amid terrible events so that you can make skillful decisions for yourself, your family, and the world.

Sometimes people think that facing the truth of a crisis and letting go of our *dukkha* means that we *approve* of it—that we accept cancer, reckless behavior, violence, oppression, or injustice. But facing the truth means knowing that something is happening that we can't avoid—and that our efforts to avoid it will make it worse. If you're reading this book, you're probably in a situation that you didn't ask for or want, and I understand how you're feeling. That's why I've shared what I've learned from my years as a Buddhist student and meditation teacher and from my own most painful experiences—when my dearest friend died of cancer, when I lived in downtown Manhattan during 9/11, and when my mother checked out of a hospital and drove straight to a tavern to start drinking again. I can tell you with certainty that you can meet this terrible moment with confidence that it will not destroy you, and you can deal with it without shame, denial, or blame. The exercises and meditations in this book will help you do it. I know intimately that it's possible to keep your heart open and your mind clear and steady even during the worst times, to develop the capacity to acknowledge and accept the ever-changing nature of life, and to discern what you can control and what you can't with openness and kindness for yourself and everyone you encounter.

That doesn't mean it will be easy. You will face many moments of great doubt—times when you feel lost, afraid, and alone, when it seems like your efforts are futile and worthless and you want to give up. That's when I hope you'll turn to this book and let me remind you of your courage—your great, brave heart—which will sustain you even in terrifying and crushing moments, when your prospects seem bleak. I know you have this courage because I have it too—we all do—and even though you might not believe right now, you will. I never thought I could be steady, calm, or brave, but using the same traditional tools I share in this book, I uncovered my great, brave heart. With a little effort, time, and practice, I'm confident that you will find yours too.

Acknowledgments

This book came about due to the efforts and encouragement of many. Thank you to:

Alice Peck, my friend, writing coach, and editor who never doubted that I could do it and who so generously contributed her talents, guidance, and expertise to make this book happen.

Eavan Cleary, for contributing her talent, vision, and time to create the beautiful cover and more.

Steven Harris, for his confidence and encouragement, and Jonathan Kurtz and the rest of the staff at Prometheus Books.

Ann Demarais and Mona Chopra, for their encouragement and enthusiasm.

Lori Piechocki and Madeleine Piechocki-Cannet, whose kindness and patience with me never wane.

My husband and greatest teacher, Michael Davey, who twice lived through the creation of this book with me.

All of the Buddhist *sangha* and its teachers, especially Sharon Salzberg and Venerable Robina Courtin.

Steady, Calm, and Brave is based on my understanding of the Buddhist teachings. I trust readers will recognize the intention of the book and the spirit in which it is offered and overlook any misinterpretations or inconsistencies due to my ignorance.

Notes on the Practices

The practices in this book are adaptations of traditional meditations that I've learned through my Buddhist training. Their purpose is to help you comfort yourself, develop insight into your habits and behavior, and ultimately free yourself from suffering.

All the practices can be adapted for anyone of any ability. If you can't walk, sit. If you can't sit, lie down. If you have asthma or breathing difficulties, use sound instead of breath to anchor yourself. Keep your eyes open or close them. There is no wrong way to meditate as long as you're present centered, paying attention, and meeting yourself with kindness.

Though everything in this book is a suggestion, not a requirement, I strongly encourage you not to skip the practices. In my experience, meditation and spending silent time alone with yourself is healing, calming, and reassuring—but only if you do it. It might be hard at first—you might be fidgety or bored—and that's okay. It takes time to get accustomed to paying attention to yourself in a new way. Don't give up—I'm confident you can do it because it was hard for me at first too, and with time and practice I'm comfortable and at ease with meditation, even on days when my mind is frustrated, dull, or filled with fast-moving thoughts.

Most importantly, be sure to use your wisdom while you're practicing. If you feel less steady and more overwhelmed, stop and try again later. If you feel too tired to meditate, take a nap. And if you're discouraged and want to quit, remember the reason you're practicing—so you can learn to take care of yourself kindly and skillfully through a difficult time and beyond.

CHAPTER 1

How Will I Get through This?

When your mind is narrow, small things agitate you very easily.
Make your mind an ocean.

—LAMA YESHE[1]

IF YOU'RE HAVING A CRISIS RIGHT NOW, IT MIGHT SEEM SURREAL. IT may have occurred so suddenly that you're in shock. Or it may have been brewing for a long time and you've been worrying about something happening, but now that it's here you can't believe it. That's how Jennifer felt. She and her husband Brian had been married for ten years, and though in many ways they were compatible—both were teachers, she taught at grammar school, he at high school—they were also often in conflict. It was so frequent that many times Jennifer thought they would separate, but each time they managed to work it out. They went to couples' counseling together and learned to be more respectful and empathetic to one another, but they always seemed to return to arguing. Finally last year, a week after Valentine's Day, at the end of another evening of shouting, it was clear to them both that they were at the point of an irretrievable breakdown. When Brian left to stay at a friend's house for the night and Jennifer heard the door close behind him, she sat down on the couch in a daze. Was she getting divorced? What would she do now? What would happen to her?

Could she find an affordable apartment? She wasn't sure what to do next and she felt scared, defeated, and lost.

You also might feel scared, defeated, and lost like Jennifer—and that's okay. The point of this book is not to try to change your emotions or tell you how to feel, but rather to help you to relate to what's happening—both internally and externally—with understanding, insight, and kindness. You can start doing this by slowing down and bringing quiet attention to your body and your heart. This might seem like the last thing you want to do when you're upset, which I understand, because most of us feel the same way. Amid a big problem or potential disaster, you probably have an urge to get things done immediately—decisions need to be made, difficulties must be fixed, and obstacles resolved. But before taking any action, it's important to take care of whatever shock, upset, or distress you're feeling so that your actions are supported by good sense, not clouded by your distress. Jennifer's first instinct was to look on the internet for an apartment, find a lawyer, and drink a glass of wine. Then she called her sister, Teri, who listened to her sobbing on the telephone and said, "Jen, just stop. You have to take care of yourself." To which Jennifer responded angrily, "I am taking care of myself! Aren't you listening to me?"

When you're in so much pain and upset that you don't know what to do about it and you just want it to stop, that's a sign to bring your attention closer to yourself. Put your hand on your chest and feel your heartbeat and your breath. Say to yourself, "I'm really struggling right now," and take ten deep, full breaths. Repeat as needed.

Taking care of yourself means listening to you. It means offering yourself your loving presence, even if the experience is deep, heavy sorrow or bitter, tight resentment. Some Buddhist teachers describe this as "making room"—when you learn to allow everything to arise in your mind and body without discrimination or judgment. *Making room* is a type of loving attention to what's actually happening inside of you, however painful it might be, and brings great relief and deep understanding.

You don't need to stop your feelings or get over them before you slow down to be with them and observe them with love. When you make room, you don't need to reject or repress any sensations that are uncomfortable or tense. You learn that your mind is spacious and can gently hold all of it—the hurt of abandonment, your impulse to lash out at others, even your self-hating thoughts and beliefs. With loving presence and openness, you realize you don't need to *do* anything about what you're experiencing, and you no longer have this type of *dukkha*—the stress and pain caused by trying to get rid of or to deny your feelings—leaving you better able to tolerate your scary, unsettling, or worrisome circumstances.

As you navigate your way through whatever crisis you're enduring, remember to take care of yourself first, before making decisions, looking for solutions, or casting recriminations so that you don't add to the struggles you're facing or make bad decisions driven by fear, desperation, or stupidity. You might not be able to prevent every unexpected danger and loss from occurring, but you can always care for yourself by making room and opening your heart to yourself through patient and loving attention to yourself, no matter what the circumstances.

You might think you don't have enough patience, kindness, or love to make room for all of the hard things in your life and in your mind. But in the Buddhist tradition, it's understood that each of us are born with a limitless capacity to care for ourselves and each other—we have all the compassion, love, joy, and wisdom that we need, and we can develop these qualities to an immeasurable capacity. We can make room in our heart for ourselves, each other, and the entire world—to love ourselves and each other indiscriminately and boundlessly.

Practice 1: Making Room

Imagine you discover an abandoned puppy on the sidewalk outside of your local drugstore on a cold night. She's shivering and hungry, pressed up against the brick wall for warmth, and you feel your heart open to her, concerned about her vulnerability, wanting to protect her and care for her. As you approach, you notice she's afraid and you want to reassure her, so you move slowly and speak softly, with great tenderness. When you reach out to touch her, she backs away, but you gently stroke her head and she relaxes, and when you pick her up and hold her against your down jacket, she clings to you fiercely and you naturally feel protective and loving toward this defenseless creature.

As you practice the following meditation, try to approach your experience just as you would a frightened and abandoned puppy. If your mind wanders and you get distracted, be patient and try again. If you get frustrated with yourself, be gentle. If you feel overwhelmed, back away, take a breath, and pause. Remember, you're a lot like this puppy—a vulnerable creature in a difficult situation who needs protection, love, and care.

1. Notice that you're upset, angry, confused, or denying that something is happening.

2. Find a comfortable place to sit and be quiet. Shut off all your devices. Close your eyes and put your hand on your belly and breathe deeply. Take at least five deep and full inhalations and exhalations.

3. Say to yourself, silently or aloud, "I'm struggling right now," "This is a hard moment for me," "I'm feeling upset," or any other words that describe what's happening inside of you.

4. Put your hand on your heart and take a few breaths. Now say, "It's okay," "I see you," "I understand," "I know you're there," or another phrase to acknowledge what's happening inside of you.

5. Keep breathing. Now say, "It's okay for this to be here," "You're welcome here," "You don't have to go away," or other words or phrases that reassure your distress, and let it know that you're not going to abandon it or yourself.

6. Keep repeating phrases as you take quiet moments, paying attention to your breath. Take deep full inhalations, and be sure to exhale fully and completely. Repeat this practice as often as you need.

CHAPTER 2

Don't Make It Worse

Free your mind. Your mind is all stories.
—DIPA MA[1]

DANIEL'S MOM BETHANY ALWAYS ASSUMED THE WORST, AND NO ONE could talk her out of it. If there was a storm, she predicted a tornado. If the car didn't start immediately, she knew she wouldn't be able to afford to fix it. And even when she was late to her job—which she'd had for six years, and the owner was her best friend, his Aunt Niki— she was sure she'd be fired. So Daniel wasn't surprised that she was inconsolable when his thirteen-year-old sister Ceci was an hour late coming home from school and they couldn't find her, even after calling all her friends and the high school. First Bethany insisted that Ceci ran away then wondered if she were lured into a car and kidnapped for sex trafficking. She imagined Ceci murdered, her body dumped by the train tracks on the other side of Dunkin' Donuts, and she called the police. As they sat in the living room waiting for an officer to arrive, Daniel said—loudly, for the third time—"Mom, she's just mad that you won't let her go to the Strokes concert! She's probably at Taco Bell with Marisa—I know she'll be home soon." Bethany shouted, "I don't know if I'll ever see her again!" and sobbed.

If you're like Bethany and your mind automatically believes the worst-case scenario in any situation, you probably have a habit of cat-

7

astrophizing. This is a common form of distorted thinking that tells us that things are much worse than they really are. Catastrophizing clouds our judgment and interferes with good decision making, and it adds unnecessary anxiety and fear to upsetting situations. If you have a tendency to immediately jump to the most terrible conclusion, you know how painful it can be for you and everyone close to you, and you even might have been told to stop doing it—but you just don't know how.

If you notice that you're not paying attention—someone said something and you didn't hear it, or you're watching a program and you missed the last ten minutes—it's a signal you're lost in your thoughts and stories. It's a good time to "stretch and sigh"—raise your hands above your head and stretch while inhaling deeply. Exhale loudly through your mouth several times.

Because catastrophizing happens so quickly, it's hard to see that it's a learned response. Dreadful thoughts arise, unbidden and unchosen, and you believe them and respond with fear and panic. But what if you didn't believe them? Thoughts aren't the same as facts or even reality—they're just a way for you to interpret and share your experiences. So you can break the cycle of catastrophic thinking by learning not to get so caught in the truth of your thoughts. One way to do this is to learn mindfulness—a simple technique of being aware of what's happening inside and outside of you in each moment. With mindfulness practice, you learn to create distance between your thoughts and your reactions and to step back and view your thoughts with interest and discernment and then choose if they are useful and truthful, whether or not you want to react to them, and how. Mindfulness is a powerful tool to lessen your investment in the delusions of worst-case scenarios or devastating fantasies and enables you to stop following them to terrible conclusions and instead come back to this very moment and what is actually happening right now.

In a calamity or crisis, one of the best things you can do for yourself and those around you is to be mindful. If you overestimate the severity of a situation with catastrophic thinking like Bethany, you won't be able to accurately measure risk or see opportunities for solutions. By the time the police arrived at Daniel's house, his mom had calmed down, and one of the officers held her hand and reassured her that in all likelihood, Ceci was fine. As she caught her breath, Bethany remembered that Niki mentioned something that morning about giving Ceci her beading kit—a big old toolbox filled with beads, wire, and other jewelry-making supplies—so she grabbed her phone and texted Niki. Yes, Ceci was there with her, and they were surprised when they learned the extent of Bethany's distress. Bethany realized that she'd allowed her fears of losing her daughter to overwhelm her and upset her so much that she couldn't even remember what she'd been told and she'd been unable to take care of herself or her children. The situation would've been much different if she had been able to notice her delusions and fears and admit them to herself instead of believing they were true.

In the Buddhist tradition, thoughts are just another of our senses. They're one of the six sense bases—*ayatana*—which include eye sense, ear sense, nose sense, mouth sense, skin/body sense, and mind sense. Each corresponds to our experiences of sight, hearing, smell, taste, touch, and thinking, all of which are important sources of information. Unfortunately, most people privilege thought over other senses like smell or taste and place the majority of their attention on mind sense, ignoring all the other information they receive. Mindfulness practice teaches us to pay attention to all our senses—to get a full picture of what's happening right now and to notice fantasies or delusions in our mind sense so we don't get caught in them.

Practice 2: Coming to Your Senses

There's a common expression that we say about someone when they do something terrible—"they were out of their senses." What we mean is that they were crazy, confused, and didn't know what they were doing—which is the opposite of mindfulness. Mindfulness is being *in* your senses—paying close attention to everything that's happening and knowing what you're doing when you're doing it. If you're mindful, you'll be able to notice when you're catastrophizing and stop yourself from jumping to a wrong conclusion and reacting foolishly, harmfully, or stupidly. It takes practice, so I suggest you do the following meditation at least once a day for six weeks and then assess your reactions in difficult moments—are you catastrophizing less?

1. Sit in a quiet room where you won't be disturbed by anyone. Set a timer on your cell phone for fifteen minutes, and put it out of your reach.

2. Make a commitment to yourself by saying silently, "I will stay here and practice until the alarm rings."

3. Close your eyes and take eight conscious breaths. Inhale fully and exhale deeply.

4. Notice what is entering each of your senses as it's happening. Examples:
   - Car horns through an open window
   - Your feet touching the carpet
   - Taste of toothpaste in your mouth
   - Smell of coffee

- Light entering through your eyelids
- Remembering a scene from a movie

5. Keep your attention lightly on your breath. You don't have to control it or make it different than it is.

6. Notice what is entering your mind sense: what thoughts or emotions are arising? Then gently return to your breath. Remember that your mind sense will include images, ideas, conversations, memories, fantasies, and plans.

7. If a thought seems very real and you like it a lot and want more of it, just notice that and choose to return to your breath. An example is thinking about what you want for dinner and imagining your options.

8. If a thought seems very real and you don't like and want it to go away, just notice that and choose to return to your breath. An example is fearing your spouse is in a car accident on the highway.

9. If you get caught in any of your thoughts, bring your attention to your breath or to another sense. Keep practicing until you hear the timer.

10. Take a few deep breaths before you rise from your seat, and thank yourself for your time and efforts.

CHAPTER 3

Living with Uncertainty

Keep Calm and Carry On
—British Propaganda Poster, 1939

"I don't know" is one of the hardest things for me to say, because not knowing makes me feel helpless, stupid, and afraid—especially in a crisis. When I don't know what's going to happen, I feel like I should either plan for the worst or insist on the best, even if I know that it's not in my control. Jenine is like that too, and after her husband Willie had a heart attack, she flew into action, researching diet plans, ordering books about heart health, and insisting that the doctors tell her exactly when he'd be discharged so she could get everything ready at home. They said that although it was a minor cardiac event and they hoped he'd be out of the hospital in a few days, they just didn't know and he needed more tests before he could leave. Jenine decided to plan a big Mother's Day celebration the following weekend at their home and invited her sons and her grandchildren. When her daughter-in-law Elmira expressed doubt that Willie would be able to attend, Jenine was angry and defensively texted her that she knew what she was doing. But when Jenine arrived at the hospital the next morning to visit Willie, the nurse stopped her before she could enter his room. She told her that he'd started running a fever, and the doctors feared an infection. His discharge was postponed, and Jenine angrily shouted "How did this happen?" "Who gave him this infection?" and "I don't understand why he isn't being released." Just then, her son Kevin entered the cardiac wing and heard his mom yelling. He ran to her, put his arms around her, and reminded her that they already knew that recovery might not be easy or quick. But all Jenine could say was, "That's not what I want!"

> If you feel yourself insisting that you know what's about to happen or what should happen, pause. Bring your attention to your body and directly experience the sensations of your feet through your feet—not by imaging your feet or thinking about your feet. Steady and regulate your breath by taking a few conscious inhalations and exhalations, and say to yourself, "I don't know and it's okay."

If you brace yourself for something horrible or anticipate a happy ending, you only cause yourself and others extra stress on top of an already stressful situation. That's because grasping at the future—insisting that circumstances will turn out the way you think they will—is inherently painful, since life is simply not predictable or in our control, and we can't count on anything except *right now*. Being here right now and paying attention to the present moment allows you to see other possibilities that could arise. Certainty is blinding—if you're sure that your house will be destroyed in the wildfire, you won't be able to also help your neighbors protect theirs. If your basement has never flooded and you know that it never will, then you'll be disappointed and unprepared for that flash flood.

If you notice, you can see that when you have a desperate need for certainty, it can lead to bad decisions, and that's why Buddhists describe wisdom as *not knowing*. Not knowing means resting in the present moment and letting go of your inclination to believe any outcome over another. Not knowing recognizes that none of us can ever fully envision the infinite outcomes of the countless incessantly changing conditions in life, but we *can* allow ourselves to pay attention to life as it unfolds moment by moment. Not knowing is what enables us to let go of anxious or fantastic certainties and instead open up to future possibilities, many of which we cannot predict.

During a crisis, if you can be levelheaded and reasonable, able to recognize that you don't know everything that will happen, then you can truly help keep others calm and prevent panic. That's because you'll be able to see clearly what needs to be done and do it. Knowing what you don't know helps you to stay steady and refrain from trying to predict the unpredictable and allows you to stay present with mindfulness and notice the often fast-moving changes presented in a crisis. Mindfulness helps you to develop trust in yourself and faith in your courage and wisdom and also to recognize the resources available to support you.

Thanks to a recent experience in which I was sure I knew something I didn't, I understand how easily someone can panic in a moment of uncertainty. I was getting an ultrasound for stomach pain and the technician was rolling a sensor back and forth across my belly. As she did so, I noticed she became very quiet and wouldn't look me in the eye. I knew she'd discovered something serious and possibly even life threatening. I started to panic and when I got home, I told my husband that I was certain I had a tumor. He said, "Kim, let's meditate for a bit before we jump to conclusions." I was upset and wasn't sure I could sit still but I knew he was right, and we sat down quietly in the living room under the Tibetan thangka painting. After a few minutes of practicing mindfulness, I noticed my breath was easier and my chest was less tight. I acknowledged that I didn't know the results of the scan, and I reassured myself that whatever they were, I would handle it and get the best treatment if needed, and my husband and family would support me. A few days later, the results showed nothing wrong. I was glad that I was able to meet my own anxiety and distress, allow myself to not know, and trust myself to deal with difficulty when it arose and not before—and I know you can too.

In many old Buddhist stories and teachings, monkeys are used to demonstrate the destructive power of an untrained mind—someone who lets their thoughts run wild. A verse in the *Dhammapada*, a collection of short teachings from early Buddhism, says:

> They run now here
> and now there,
> as if looking for fruit:
> a monkey in the forest.[1]

Like monkeys who swing from one branch to the next, whose attention dashes from one object to another, and who can't stop chattering or slow down, when you have a "monkey mind," your mind wildly races from thought to thought, you can't focus your attention, and you're unsettled, restless, and unable to relax. Mindfulness and meditation are trainings designed to calm this "monkey mind" through benevolent discipline and gentle persistence so you can settle down, make good decisions, and bring kindness to your struggles.

Practice 3: Steady Mind

During a big change like a crisis, you might notice that you're distracted, forgetful, or ruminating, unable to pay attention or be present for what's really happening because you're too afraid of what might happen in the future. Maybe you lost your keys and found them in your pocket where you left them or discover you haven't heard a thing your colleague told you about a meeting. It's important, especially during a difficult time, to keep your mind and attention steady and focused on the present moment so that you can see, hear, and consider new and changing information and respond appropriately with wisdom and compassion for yourself and everyone around you. Try practicing this exercise several times a day to steady your mind and pay attention to what's really happening.

1. Find a quiet place where you will be undisturbed for at least ten minutes.

2. Shut off your devices and sit down.

3. Close your eyes and take five deep, slow, even breaths.

4. Notice any emotions and ideas that you might have, especially those about the uncertain future. You might be imagining disasters and tragedy or feeling a sense of doom, terror, or nervousness, and that's okay. Keep breathing and don't let yourself get caught up in the story. Know that whatever you're feeling is okay, and you're not alone.

5. Now take a moment to bring your attention to your body sensations and feel what's happening. Perhaps your stomach is growling or tense, you're grinding your teeth, or you're feeling

cold or warm. Just notice with kindness, and don't try to change or fix anything about yourself—nothing is wrong with you, and no problem needs to be solved right now.

6. Breathe deeply and say, "This is the way things are right now and I'm okay." You can put your hand on your heart as you repeat this phrase to yourself. Keep your attention on what you're experiencing right now—your body, thoughts, and emotions. Offer yourself the same patience as you would give a friend.

7. Continue noticing and paying kind attention to yourself, repeating the steps above as needed.

8. Stay for the full ten minutes. At the end of your practice, before you open your eyes, put your hand on your heart or your belly and silently wish yourself and the world safety and peace.

CHAPTER 4

Suffering Is Not a Dirty Word

Pain is inevitable. Suffering is optional.
—Haruki Murakami[1]

PEOPLE WHO DON'T KNOW MUCH ABOUT BUDDHISM SOMETIMES think that it's a depressing religion because of its focus on suffering. But what they don't know or understand is that this is because we *are* all suffering. We're all suffering because we're deeply resistant to the way things are—to the fact that all of us will get older, get sick, and die, that we'll lose everything we love, and that we have little control over it. This is the pain of *dukkha*—the suffering caused by our deep resistance to and dissatisfaction with life.

Each moment that you don't want life to be the way it is, you're suffering—you have *dukkha*. If your life is going smoothly without disruptions right now, your *dukkha* is likely small and uncomfortable, revealing itself as dissatisfaction. When I went downstairs to get the mail this morning, which was late and hadn't arrived yet, I felt annoyed that I would have to walk downstairs again later to pick it up—that was *dukkha*. When my cat spilled a glass of water and I was irritated, that was *dukkha*. But during a crisis, when you're experiencing the heartbreak of loss, danger, or uncertainty—that's when your *dukkha* is more obvious, and you have an opportunity to truly understand it and let go of it.

If you feel a big "no" welling up inside of you—a feeling of "this is wrong, it shouldn't be happening, I don't want this to be true"—that's a moment of *dukkha*. Take a deep breath and notice your resistance to what's happening, and bring kindness and attention to what you're experiencing inside—the fear, frustration, sadness, or neediness you're feeling.

When Derrick's partner, Jimmy, was diagnosed with emphysema, Derrick stared at the doctor defiantly and told him, "We're getting a second opinion!" They did, and when the second doctor confirmed what the first said, Derrick said nothing and walked out of the office. He was so angry that he couldn't sleep and kept telling Jimmy, his friends, and his colleagues at work that this "shouldn't be happening." He saw his therapist a week later and told her the same thing. "But it is happening," she said, "and you must be in so much pain."

In the Buddhist tradition, there's no way out of your human experience. When you believe or act like it's possible to stop things from changing, to not grow old, or to avoid getting sick, you cause yourself tremendous *dukkha*. *Dukkha* is caused by *avidya*—our deep ignorance and denial of the nature of life. When you embrace the poignant truth of impermanence and stop trying to control what you can't control, this ignorance transforms to wisdom, and you'll alleviate your *dukkha*. Then you can bring your deepest compassion to your pain and struggles, which are much easier to bear without your resistance and denial. When the Vietnamese Zen master Thich Nhat Hanh said, "happiness is here and now,"[2] he didn't mean that we would feel cheerful and excited all the time. He meant that even in times of sorrow and pain, we can let go of our *dukkha* and bring our kindness, our attention, and our love to ourselves and pay attention to our unhappiness. We don't have to fight our suffering or get rid of it—we can bring peace to what we're experiencing and have unhappiness with happiness at the same time.

Derrick realized that he didn't want to believe Jimmy was sick because it made him feel helpless and stupid. As an engineer he'd spent his life fixing problems, and he was ashamed that he couldn't solve this one. When he accepted that curing Jimmy was not in his power, he understood Jimmy's illness not as proof of his own inadequacies, but rather as evidence of the truth of Derrick's own humanity and deep ability to feel and care. He stopped fighting the diagnosis and let himself feel his terror at losing his love, his appreciation for their beautiful life together, and the poignancy of accepting the vulnerability and brevity of life.

> *Right View* is one of the practices that help free us from *dukkha*. It's part of the Eightfold Path—sometimes translated as "the way to the end of suffering." The Eightfold Path are fundamental Buddhist disciplines leading to liberation from suffering. Practicing Right View means seeing the basic laws of reality clearly—including that everything in our life is always changing and that we don't have control over it all. Right View helps us remember that we can use our speech and behavior to benefit ourselves and others, even in difficult moments. If you can be guided by Right View, then whatever you do or say will naturally lead toward harmony with yourself and others, unobscured by the inability to see the truth of life (*avidya*) or the pain you feel because of it (*dukkha*).

Practice 4: Saying Yes

Sometimes when I'm upset, I feel a terrible tightness in my chest, as if something is strangling my heart. I've learned that this is a sign that I don't want to believe what's happening—that the photos of the flooded streets in my neighborhood aren't really that bad or that the policeman is wrong about how terrible the accident was. I've learned that this is how my *dukkha* manifests sometimes, and the best way to alleviate it is to notice it and allow it. You can identify your *dukkha* too. It will feel different at different times. Use the following practice to notice it and help you ease your resistance and open your heart to your pain, worry, and upset.

1. Shut off your devices and stop talking. Find a quiet spot where you won't be disturbed, then get still and take a few deep breaths.

2. Decide to stay here, feeling your urge to fight, resist, oppose, or stop something that is happening. Notice any impulse or wish to solve, fix, or cure. Feel the sensations of your body—you might experience tension around your chest, coldness in your abdomen or genitals, shaking legs, or sweaty palms. This is a sign of your *dukkha*. Whatever it is, just let yourself be with it.

3. Put your hand on your belly, experiencing your inhalations and exhalations. As you breathe in, say to yourself, "Yes." As you breathe out, say to yourself, "Yes." Continue repeating this silently as you breathe, giving yourself permission to drop any resistance to what's happening and to let yourself open to the reality of your situation.

4. Take your time and continue for at least five minutes or as long as you like. Conclude your practice by taking a minute to thank yourself for your kindness, wisdom, and effort.

CHAPTER 5

Hope and Trust

I have come to trust the true freedom of living where the moon does not dwell.

—Roshi Merle Kodo Boyd[1]

BRANDON'S MOM WAS EIGHTY-FIVE YEARS OLD AND LIVED ALONE IN a sixty-and-older housing community. A retired physical therapist, she'd always been active at her church and with her walking group, and for a long time she was the copresident of her local League of Women Voters. But Brandon and his sister noticed that she was becoming more forgetful and avoiding their phone calls. She also wasn't going out much anymore. When they asked her about it, she said she just preferred to stay home. But they were unprepared when her longtime general practitioner, Dr. Gage, called to tell them that their mother had hydrocephalus and needed surgery immediately. She was conscious but confused and unable to authorize the surgery. Brandon was her healthcare proxy—would he give his permission to insert a shunt to drain the pressure on her brain? His first instinct was to say, "Yes, of course," but then he questioned himself—is that what his mom would want? There was a small risk of complications, and she'd always been clear that she didn't want to be on life support or to live with a poor quality of life. He discussed it with his sister and talked to the doctor again, and after reassurance that the surgery would likely be successful, he finally agreed to sign the authorization papers. But he truly wasn't sure if he'd made the right decision. He saw his sister at the hospital the next day and told her how concerned he was about making a bad decision. He felt relieved when she said, "There is no bad decision—you made the best possible choice with the information you had. That's all you can do."

In a crisis, you'll have to make difficult and uncertain decisions too, and, like Brandon, you'll need to trust yourself and hope for a positive outcome. In Buddhism, hope and trust are linked—hope means trusting that you and everyone else will do your very best in the most difficult moments. Cultivating a sense of hope and trust means having faith in yourself and developing confidence in your wisdom and compassion to guide you to make skillful choices. It might feel strange to have faith in yourself, but you can be sure you've made hard decisions many times before. Each time you've been in a difficult situation, you've found your way through it. Maybe you made the painful choice to break up with a long-term partner or risked your career on a new job in a new industry. Whatever the situation was—no matter if the results were auspicious or not—you can trust that you'll use your best judgment and good sense time and time again, in any situation.

> If you're feeling overwhelmed and about to give up, take a moment to feel your struggle and pain. Put your hand on your heart, take a few breaths, and say to your hurt and fear, "I'm here for you. I'm not leaving you. We will get through this."

Hope and trust also include knowing that you're not the only one who has experienced health problems, disasters, and unexpected events—all people have gone through them, and they've done their best despite terrible conditions and so will you. With mindfulness and compassion, you can discover your inner wisdom and courage to support yourself and others, and perhaps you'll even experience post-traumatic growth and resilience. This happened to Kelly, and it surprised her. When she went to an outdoor concert and a gunman began firing into the crowd, she ran, holding hands with her little brother, Tomas, but they didn't get far before they stumbled and fell to the ground. Kelly noticed she'd lost her right shoe, her foot was covered in blood, and she'd been shot in the lower leg. Since she couldn't walk without assistance, Tomas dragged her, and Kelly leaned on him as they hurried out of the venue. A stranger stopped them, took off his belt, and tied it around Kelly's thigh to staunch the bleeding. A woman in a pickup truck pulled over and Tomas and Kelly got in the back with several other terrified concertgoers, and they sped to the hospital, where the emergency room staff treated her injury. It took months before Kelly felt safe in public spaces again, and she still suffers from post-traumatic stress disorder when she hears loud noises. But she feels grateful for Tomas and the rest of her supportive family, has a true understanding and appreciation that there are kind strangers all around her, and is relieved to know that she can trust her good sense and strength even in the most terrifying situation.

Sometimes when I'm in a stressful or scary place, I forget to trust myself. Instead, I wish and hope for someone to come and rescue me and fix things or make it all better—and make *me* feel better. But when that doesn't happen, I feel so discouraged that I just want to get into bed and hide. I've learned that I don't need to do that anymore. With practice and trust in myself, I've learned that *I* can be the one I'm hoping for—*I* can trust myself to offer comfort, love, kindness, and patience to myself and my hopelessness and to use my wisdom to remember my strengths and blessings too. And you can be the one you're hoping for, too.

Start by remembering that it's okay to acknowledge that your circumstances are truly hard right now. You can recognize whatever is happening—that you're unsure of yourself, that you might lose someone you love, that you're in danger—because it's the truth. It's also the truth that you have support and care too. And even if you don't feel them right now, it's important for you to keep a clear and wide perspective of both your impediments and your advantages. If you see only the struggles, you'll get discouraged and fall into despair. And if you focus only on the good things, you won't be able to face your problems clearly and respond to them appropriately. Then be sure to remember all you've given and received throughout your lifetime. You can do this with the practice at the end of this chapter, which will reconnect you to your good heart, reestablish your connection with others, and ground you in the truth of life—that you can trust that all circumstances—good, bad, or neutral—are impermanent and inevitably will change and end.

> *Saddha* is translated as conviction, trust, or faith in the Buddha and his teachings, but also in ourselves and our capacity to awaken. People with great *saddha* are especially courageous and wise because their conviction enables them to be a refuge not only for themselves, but for others. Their trust inspires confidence in others to cultivate the same. In the *Saddha Sutta*,[2] the Buddha says: "Just as a large banyan tree, on level ground where four roads meet, is a haven for the birds all around, even so a lay person of conviction is a haven for many people: monks, nuns, male lay followers, and female lay followers."

Practice 5: Gladden Your Mind

During times of stress and difficulty, it's easy to become so focused on the problems that are happening that you might forget any goodness, support, and love you have in yourself and in your life. But even if you can't feel them right now, they exist, though they may be things that you take for granted: the thoughtful texts your best friend sends you or your own kindness in making lunch for your child. If you're struggling right now, take a few minutes before each meal to practice gladdening your mind with this easy exercise.

1. Sit down and take a few breaths and make a commitment to yourself to stay here for five minutes.

2. Close your eyes and remember something you thought, said, did, or experienced recently that was beneficial, kind, generous, or wise.

3. This might include a text you sent to check on your niece who's out of work and job hunting; it could be when you hugged someone who needed it or when you took time to eat breakfast instead of just drinking coffee all morning.

4. You can include events from the past too, like the time in first grade when you stopped your best friend from killing a spider and released it outdoors or ten years ago when you prayed for your sick grandmother.

5. Now include the kindnesses and support you've received from others. Start with recent experiences, which could be small, like getting information from the National Weather Service or helpful emails from your child's teacher. Then you can include

past moments too, remembering so many times when family, friends, or strangers showed you love, kindness, or care. It might be something like when you were ten years old fishing by yourself and a stranger helped you untangle your line or last month when your local pharmacist filled your prescription for you right away so you wouldn't have to wait until the next day.

Try to do this practice each morning. It will stop your mind from immediately falling into negative and hopeless patterns and provide you with more balance. It's important to see both problems and goodness clearly so that we can meet our lives with resilience and wisdom. You can also do this as a journaling exercise, writing down all that you remember.

CHAPTER 6

Love Yourself

Love allows us to enter paradise. Still, many of us wait outside the gates, unable to cross the threshold.

—BELL HOOKS[1]

IN THE BUDDHIST TRADITION, *METTA*—A PALI WORD TRANSLATED AS loving-kindness or love—is seen as a powerful force, one that leads to sharing, healing, and cooperation among living beings. It's necessary for all successful relationships, for harmonious societies, and for a healthy planet. The main point of *metta*—maybe the single most liberating realization from practicing it—is that everybody wants to be happy, deserves to be happy, and is doing all kinds of confused, ignorant, and even dangerous things, all in the hope of becoming happy. "Everybody" includes your family and neighbors. It includes dogs, cockroaches, giraffes, and minnows. It includes animals that I eat, strangers on the subway, dangerous leaders, and people I dislike. It includes you and your relationship to yourself. The foundation of *metta* practice is truly wishing yourself happiness and freedom from *dukkha*—the suffering we cause ourselves when we resist and avoid what's really happening.

> The easiest way to develop *metta* is to simply put your hand on your heart, think of yourself, everyone you know, and strangers all over the world and say, "May we all be safe and happy."

Practicing *metta* for yourself is the same as developing self-compassion or self-love. It means showing yourself kindness and care, especially in times of struggle or upset. It means offering yourself wise support and encouragement and recognizing you're not alone. Giving yourself compassion and love isn't selfish or exclusive because caring about yourself gives you the necessary strength, fortitude, and resilience to meet your difficulties without burning out or falling apart.

Cindy knew she needed to find a way to give herself love after the tornado struck. During the storm, she and her kids sheltered in the utility room, the most secure part of the house, which had a concrete floor and cinderblock walls. They watched as the morning light faded, the sky grew dark, and a deathly roar filled their ears—then it was over. Cindy peeked outside and when she saw it was clear, they went outside. As they looked over their home and driveway, the only damage they could see was two broken windows and the mangled backyard fence. But she could see that one neighbor's house and car were in ruins and another had lost their garage. Cindy sat down at the kitchen table and thought about all the work it would take for her neighbors to repair their property and silently sent them prayers of strength and love to get through it. When her daughter Sophie came in to check if the water was working, she said, "Mom, your hands are shaking." That's when Cindy realized she was struggling too, still in shock from the storm and wondering how she'd afford a new fence. She took a deep breath and offered strength and love to herself.

If you're not accustomed to giving yourself love and kindness, it might feel awkward or strange, and that's okay. You also might think you don't have enough *metta* for yourself, that you have only a small amount of it, so you can give only a little bit to this person and a little bit to that one and there isn't any left over for you. But you're wrong. Your capacity for *metta* is boundless, and the more you practice it, the more you have to give. Instead of being stingy with your *metta*, you can give your loving-kindness generously to yourself and still have plenty to include everyone else too.

From a Buddhist view, you never need to exclude yourself from your circle of love and care, because you're as worthy of it as anyone else. The great Indian Buddhist teacher Shantideva[2] called this "equalizing self and other," because he noticed that we tend to think of ourselves as either less deserving than someone we think is better or nicer than we are or more deserving than someone we think is worse or less good than we are. When you equalize yourself with other people, you recognize that we're all the same—struggling humans doing our best to be happy, even if we make mistakes or cause harm sometimes.

Practice 6: Learning to Love

Metta meditation is a traditional Buddhist meditation practice described in early teachings and detailed in the *Vishidimagga*, or *Path of Purification*. It's designed to help develop concentration, wisdom, and the quality of *metta*, which includes all forms of love. What follows is an abbreviated *metta* meditation, one that you can easily do anytime that you feel burnt out, upset, or scared and want to restore your relationship with yourself or someone else.

1. Find a quiet spot where you can be undisturbed for just five minutes.

2. Notice your feet on the floor, feel your breath and the air on your skin. Put your hand on your belly and let it move with the rise and fall of your respiration.

3. Make a connection by imagining someone close to you and silently say to them, *May you care for yourself with ease, may you be open to the way things are, may you be free.* Continue saying this silently for a few minutes.

4. Then connect with yourself and give yourself the same silent wishes, *May I care for myself with ease, may I be open to the way things are, may I be free.*

5. Finally, include all of us struggling beings on our ecosystem called Earth, *May we care for ourselves with ease, may we be open to the way things are, may we be free.*

6. End the meditation by sitting silently for just a minute or two. Then, before you move or stand, be sure to say thank you to yourself in appreciation for your wisdom and good sense.

CHAPTER 7

Living with Grief and Loss

It is only because of change that suffering can end—and it is because of change that our bodies fall apart, like all compounded things. We cannot have one without the other, but we try.
—SALLIE TISDALE[1]

IF YOU'RE READING THESE WORDS, YOU'VE PROBABLY EXPERIENCED or are about to experience a loss. You might feel sad, disheartened, or crushed, and I understand—not only because I remember what it was like when my mom died and I know how awful I felt when I got fired, but simply because all of us live with the upset of change and impermanence. The grief and mourning you feel are natural responses to your situation, but you might not want to feel them because they're so painful and because few of us have been taught to expect loss and honor grief.

Expecting loss means that you understand that nothing is permanent. The truth of human life is that each one of us will experience loss and death, and we usually don't know when or how. You might think—like I do—"Of course I know that," but then when you hear that Kobe Bryant died in a helicopter crash, you're shocked, or when your favorite restaurant suddenly closes, you can't believe it. Both reactions reveal your resistance to and denial of the impermanence of all things. When you can accept that loss is inevitable, you'll have more appreciation of life and be more at peace with the unexpected. You'll be able to honor your grief and face it instead of avoiding or denying it or getting angry and looking to blame someone or something for it.

A crisis means a change, and change inevitably includes loss. If you're in pain and sad right now, you might be bereaved. This is a normal response to sudden calamity. If you notice you're ignoring or dismissing your grief, stop for a moment, put your hand on your heart, and take a few deep breaths. Feel your feet on the ground and say to yourself, "I'm here and it's okay to feel this way."

Honoring grief means allowing yourself to feel your sorrow without pushing it away or ignoring it. You might think that you don't have time to deal with your pain or that you shouldn't feel so bad because other people have worse problems than yours, or you could be waiting impatiently for your sadness to disappear and for things to go back to normal, like Sharifa. A year after her dad died in a car accident, she still didn't want to face her anguish; it was just too hard and she didn't know how to endure the pain she felt. She'd heard and read on the internet and in books that her grief would be less acute over time, but it wasn't. She was barely getting through each day, counting the hours and waiting for the time when her sorrow would dissipate and her old self would return. Sometimes she was enraged that the driver who caused the crash wasn't charged with a crime or felt guilty that she didn't ask her dad to take a different route to work that day. She fantasized about going back in time to sabotage his car so the accident would never happen. She finally called Alex, a former colleague whose brother had died unexpectedly of appendicitis a decade before. She demanded to know how long it would be until she felt better. He said he didn't know because his pain never really went away. He said he'd learned to make room for it and accept it and even appreciate it, and now it didn't upset him so much anymore. He suggested Sharifa stop wishing and wanting her grief to end, but this wasn't what she had hoped to hear, and when the call ended, she was annoyed. Yet, to her surprise, soon after their conversation, she felt relieved. She noticed that when she dropped her resistance to what was happening—heartbreak and loneliness—she experienced less stress and intolerance of her emotions and expectations and could let herself relax into these feelings without wanting them to disappear.

Sharifa and Alex learned to understand their *dukkha*—the additional suffering caused by wanting their grief to end. What they learned is that it's easier to open to their pain than to push it away, and you can learn to do this too. Maybe you lost your job, your savings, or your home, or someone you love has recently died or is about to die. You can acknowledge how terrible and painful and sad it is and choose to embrace your sorrow and bring kindness to your broken heart. This will help you feel less alone with your sadness, better able to bear your grief with compassion, and more resilient to the tragedies and shocks that will inevitably occur in your life and in all of our lives.

Many people think that becoming a Buddhist means that they won't have any more difficult feelings—that with meditation and training, nothing in the world will affect them. This is because they commonly mistake indifference for equanimity, but they're not the same at all. Indifference means not caring or having concern and refusing to let oneself be affected even by the most painful and sad experiences. Equanimity means keeping steadfast even in the midst of difficulty. It's a quality that enables us to accept that everything changes and is impermanent. Then we don't have to resist loss, and we can let ourselves be affected by everything that happens—the good, the bad, and the boring—without turning away or ignoring it. Equanimity lets us care about the sadness of the world without getting overwhelmed or discouraged.

Practice 7: Finding Peace

When I first tried this meditation, I thought it was silly to tell myself to have peace when I didn't feel peaceful at all. You might think that too—or that repeating the phrases won't really do anything for you or make you feel differently than you do. Although it's true that meditation takes practice and you might have to try it daily for a while before you notice its effects, it's also true that directing your thoughts toward peace, caring, and wisdom will rewire destructive habits of mind—like a tendency to dwell on difficulty or ruminate on loss—and create new, more constructive pathways over time. So give this meditation a try and don't worry if it feels awkward or if you have doubts. I practiced it for a few weeks and didn't notice any change until one day while riding on the subway, the train abruptly stopped in a tunnel. There was a mechanical problem and we were stuck there for nearly an hour. I was late for a meeting and getting angrier and angrier when a voice in my head said, "May I be open to the changes in life. May I be at peace." I laughed to myself and realized it was nothing more than an unexpected delay that would end, and thirty minutes later it did.

1. Find a quiet place, get still, and take a few deep exhalations and inhalations. Then put your hand on your heart.

2. Make a connection with yourself. You can visualize yourself—as you appear when you look in the mirror or maybe during a moment from your childhood—or simply have a sense of your loving presence. Then say these sentences silently to yourself: *May I be open to the changes in life. May I be at peace.* Repeat each sentence as though you're giving it as a gift to yourself.

3. After a few minutes, include someone else who is experiencing loss. You might imagine this person is sitting with you, or you

can evoke a sense of the two of you together. Then say this silently to you both: *May we be open to the changes in life. May everyone be at peace.*

4. Finally, you can share your good heart and wisdom by imagining all the people all over the world struggling right now with a crisis, a disaster, or an unexpected calamity, and say to all: *May we be open to the changes in life. May everyone be at peace.*

5. After a few minutes, you can stop repeating the phrases. Just let yourself stay still, with your eyes closed, and rest here for a few minutes before you get up. Don't forget to say "thank you" to yourself for your skillful efforts.

CHAPTER 8

When Your Family Is Making You Crazy

A dysfunctional family is any family with more than one person in it.

—MARY KARR[1]

AFTER JOHN AND EDUARDO'S TWELVE-YEAR-OLD SON TOBIAS cracked his head open at the skate park, they both decided to work from home while he recovered. A grade 4 concussion meant Tobias needed to stay home and rest, remain quiet, and limit his time on computers, televisions, and cell phones. John and Eduardo took turns playing checkers and reading to him, and after being at home together twenty-four hours a day for five days, John realized that his husband was the most annoying person in the world. Eduardo wouldn't listen to anything he said, took his socks off and left them under his desk in the living room, and refused to admit when he was wrong. John was irritated any time he had to interact with him—until John realized Eduardo was just as irritated interacting with *him*. One night after Tobias fell asleep, Eduardo abruptly told John *he* was the most annoying person in the world. He said John didn't listen to anything he said, borrowed his headphones and didn't return them, and refused to admit when he was wrong. John was surprised and shared that he was feeling the same way about Eduardo, and they both laughed. They recognized how scared they were about Tobias and that they were projecting their fears and anxieties onto each other instead of talking about their concerns together.

Life during a crisis is stressful and upsetting. It disrupts our normal routines, and suddenly we might find ourselves spending all our time with the same people in our homes or together visiting someone in a hospital room with only one chair for three or four people. Our work and school might be disrupted, so we don't get a break from our partner or family like we usually do when we separate and go to our respective jobs and do our individual errands, walks, playdates, and all our other regular activities. While Tobias recovered, Eduardo's workplace and computer monitors took up living room space and John's desk cluttered their bedroom, and their entire home seemed a lot smaller—their whole life seemed to have shrunk. If you're in the midst of a crisis, dealing with partners, spouses, children, and extended family members—no matter how much you love them—is not easy.

> If you feel upset with someone, it's okay. But before you say something to them, take a few breaths, let your heart rate slow and your body calm down. Then you can choose what you're going to say instead of impulsively speaking without thinking.

When Margo and Tony's building in Milwaukee caught fire, they lost everything. Faulty wiring in the kitchen below them sparked a flame in the walls that quickly made its way up to their apartment. The fire department arrived swiftly, and they were evacuated with their neighbors. No one was injured but more than fifteen families were displaced. Margo and Tony stayed with their daughter Cristy, her husband, and their six-year-old twin daughters in suburban Brookfield. It was only temporary—though their building was uninhabitable and they wouldn't be able to move back in, with their landlord's insurance and their savings, they were looking for a new place. But tensions started to reveal themselves immediately. Margo insisted on cooking bacon and eggs for the girls every morning, frustrating their parents who didn't eat much meat. Tony felt insulted by his son-in-law Michael, who wouldn't let him fix the basement sink, even though he was a pretty good plumber and had successfully done many such repairs in the past. Margo decided that instead of assuming that she was helping her daughter, she would give her more space. She and Tony went for walks and out for dinner alone a few times a week, and when they moved to a condo in Fox Point a few months later, she was glad they still were close with Cristy and Michael.

If you feel irritated, frustrated, or just tired of your closest family and friends right now, it's okay. Do your best to create private time— go for a walk, close the door to your bedroom and take a nap, sit in your backyard, listen to music through headphones. It's important to rest and relax by yourself even if it's only for a short amount of time. If you're a parent with small children who can't be left unattended, this may be harder for you. Do your best to share responsibilities with your partner (if you have one) so that each of you has time to yourselves and take advantage of naptime.

If other people are irritated, frustrated, or just tired from being around you, that's okay too. It doesn't mean you've done anything wrong. Don't pressure them to tell you why they're upset or demand they feel differently. Give them space and allow them to have their feelings. Just like you, they're struggling with this situation. By offering your patience and openness to whatever they're experiencing, you'll help them feel supported and loved.

Remember: if you do get angry at your partner, child, family member, friend, it's okay; it's a normal feeling. But if you feel hostile or aggressive or your anger drives you to want to scream, fight, insult anyone, or even lash out in a passive-aggressive way, it's not okay. Sit down and feel your anger. You don't have to get rid of it, but you don't have to act out of it either. It might have been triggered by another person, but it's yours and only you can take care of it.

There's an old Buddhist teaching called "The Insult,"[2] in which the Buddha is walking through a village, and a local man who doesn't like the Buddha or his teachings chases after him and yells rudely and insults him, calling him a fraud and an idiot. The Buddha stops and calmly asks the man, "If you gave me a gift and I didn't accept it, who would own it?" The man, bewildered, says, "me." The Buddha is telling him to keep his anger. He says:

> In the same way, brahman, that with which you have insulted me, who is not insulting; that with which you have taunted me, who is not taunting; that with which you have berated me, who is not berating: that I don't accept from you. It's all yours, brahman. It's all yours.

The Buddha knows that we don't have to be tied to the whim of another's behavior. No matter how difficult your family and friends might be, you can keep your feet firm and your mind steady and refuse any "gift" of anger, frustration, or annoyance that you're given and let it remain with the giver, not you.

Practice 8: I See You, Anger

Anger has a lot of energy, which is why it's hard to simply sit down and feel it when you have it. You might have to practice the first step in this meditation many times before you even get to the second step—and that's okay. Remember, it takes patience and diligence to learn new habits. Be kind to yourself and have confidence, because if I can do it, I know you can too.

1. Disengage, stop talking, and separate yourself from the conflict—go to another room, sit in your car, or walk around the block.

2. Deeply inhale through your nose, bringing air all the way to your belly and exhale slowly. Do this at least three times.

3. Notice that you're angry and what that feels like in your body. Your heart may be racing, you might have lots of fast and mean thoughts arising, you may have a tight jaw or clenched fists or an upset stomach. It's all okay—you don't have to fix or change anything.

4. Keep paying attention. As you inhale, say, "I see my anger," and as you breathe out, say, "I'm here for you, anger."

5. Repeat these instructions until you feel calmer and less reactive. You might need to return to a step or start over again and that's okay. Don't give up.

6. Before you stop practicing and resume your activities, recognize that it's challenging to work with the energy of anger. Be sure to thank yourself for your efforts.

CHAPTER 9

Watching a Crisis Unfold

Whether you graduate from Harvard Law School or you graduate from college, whether you're a social worker or a teacher, you should not underestimate the power you have to affirm the humanity and dignity of the people who are around you.

—BRYAN STEVENSON[1]

DURING A DISASTER OR A CRISIS, IT CAN BE SO CHALLENGING TO know what to do. Unless you have the special skills of a nurse or an emergency medical technician or are a professional relief worker, you may feel awful, not being able to help as you watch people in need suffer. I felt this way after 9/11 in New York City when the World Trade Center was attacked. The day after, I went with friends to Union Square Park and watched helplessly as family members searched for their loved ones, posting hundreds of missing person flyers on every available surface—fences, benches, railings—in and around the park. As we watched the smoke rising from downtown, we felt defeated and impotent. Decades later, I felt the same way when my husband and I watched the news of Russia's attacks on Ukraine, hearing and reading firsthand accounts of the devasting violence and the hardship of so many refugees trying to find their way to safety. I remembered Thrangu Rinpoche,[2] a Tibetan teacher who encourages us to recognize that even if it feels like we can't do anything to help in a terrible situation, we can always offer love and compassion. This can benefit some people immediately, others gradually, and some only in the far-off future, but offering love and compassion is never wasted or foolish.

> If you're in a crisis and you feel like there's nothing you can do, you're wrong. You can always bring your kindness, concern, and awareness to those in need. Close your eyes, feel your helplessness, and silently say to all who need it, "May you be safe and unafraid." Repeat as needed.

Wisdom is knowing when a collective or personal crisis cannot be cured or resolved on our own. Even with lots of other people or plenty of money, some problems simply can't be fixed. But that doesn't mean we do nothing. With our love and kindness, we can actively choose to witness the suffering of friends, neighbors, and strangers so that they are not alone and their struggles are not ignored. This reminds us that our deep connection to all living beings is undeniable, and far from being helpless, we can use any disaster as a profound opportunity to recognize and honor our interdependent lives. We can also choose to educate ourselves, to give, act, and donate as we can, and to affect local, state, and federal politics and legislation so that future beings suffer less.

Love is a type of wisdom acknowledging that each of us is a vulnerable, confused being who truly wants to be happy and free from suffering. It's also a skill you can develop, a power you can learn with practice and effort, to create a circle of care that includes everyone—you, your family, friends, strangers, people you like, and people you don't like. Love includes even dangerous people—we keep them in our hearts so that we're not filled with hatred, so that we can do our utmost with a clear mind and stop them from doing more injury or harm.

Practicing love during a crisis means being receptive to your own fears and hopes, as well as with people you know who are scared or angry. You can be mindful and careful with your words and refrain from harsh communication to create less panic and divisiveness, to help your community come together, and to make a difficult time as easy as possible. You can lovingly notice your own greed and neediness and choose to act instead from generosity and a spirit of giving. You can also pay attention to what leaders are saying and doing, support those who are competent, compassionate, and effective in safeguarding all citizens and alleviating the economic strain that results for so many when disaster strikes. You'll see for yourself that acting with love is a powerful force for good and helps to create the conditions of insight and attention needed to make real connections and lasting change.

Buddhists refer to destructive emotions as afflictions, painful mind-states, or poisons. That's because they harm *you*—they damage your ability to think clearly and behave appropriately with wisdom and love. The Three Poisons, also called the "Three Unwholesome Roots," are hatred, greed, and delusion. They're the ultimate cause of all the problems in the world. War, poverty, environmental degradation, racism, sexism, and other forms of oppression are the result of actions rooted in these three poisonous mind-states. That's why Buddhist teachings emphasize the opposite qualities—*metta* (loving-kindness or love), generosity, and wisdom—so that we can use them as antidotes and liberate ourselves from our afflictive and harmful emotions.

Practice 9: Opening Your Heart to the World

It might seem too overwhelming to widen your circle of care to include anyone beyond your close friends and family, but it's actually quite freeing. When you include everyone, then you don't have to tightly protect your heart and guard your love and wisdom. You can surrender and open to your boundless capacity for love and share it without discrimination. When you embrace the world with your great brave heart, you're simply remembering your deepest insight and clarity—that you're connected to all living beings and that all living beings are connected to you.

1. Begin by finding a quiet place where you can be undisturbed. If you're at home, ask your roommates and family members to give you some privacy for ten minutes.

2. Sit still, close your eyes or gaze softly at the ground, and put your hand on your heart.

3. Take a few deep breaths.

4. Imagine you're connecting with you. You can imagine you're looking in the mirror and silently say these phrases to yourself: *May I be safe and healthy. May I be happy and free.* Repeat them, like a gift you're giving yourself, for a few minutes.

5. Next, imagine someone you know personally or indirectly who is actively helping during a crisis—a friend who is an EMT, a nurse or social worker, an activist or community organizer.

Silently say the phrases to this person for a few minutes: *May you be safe and healthy. May you be happy and free.*

6. Finally, include all beings everywhere—in your community, state, country, and all the other nations on Earth—remembering that we're all connected. Give your generous and indiscriminate love and compassion to everyone by repeating these phrases: *May we be safe and healthy. May we be happy and free.* Say thank you to yourself before you conclude this practice, appreciating your willingness to open your heart and share your kindness with yourself and others.

CHAPTER 10

Just Relax

The plants and flowers I raised about my hut I now surrender
To the will
Of the wind

—Ryōkan[1]

My friend Alice—whose son is now a young adult—told me that during a crisis she has to work through a deeper feeling than fear, something that she calls "mother fear"—an unshakable dread that, no matter what she does, she won't be able to keep her family and the people she loves safe. She's terrified that they're doomed and that someone—maybe everyone—will die, and she's unable to sleep, eat, or think of anything else. She's learned that when she has this feeling, it's a sign she needs to relax.

Relaxing was the last thing I wanted to do or thought I needed during times of dread and doom in my life—like when my alcoholic mother had a car accident or during Hurricane Sandy—but surrendering to my fears and worries has been a surprisingly effective way to lessen them. I remembered this recently after my twenty-year-old niece was exposed to the measles at the airport when she returned from a weekend holiday in Tulum. She was contacted by health officials who said that a person with the disease was on her flight. I wasn't too worried about her—she was young and vaccinated—but she'd had dinner with her mother, Tanya, and her grandmother, Mildred, the night she got home. Tanya had a compromised immune system and Mildred was one hundred years old—so both would be in danger if they contracted measles, a serious disease that could even be fatal. Like Alice, I was frightened and spent several sleepless nights worrying and fearing they would get sick. I felt helpless and was filled with dread. But when I noticed how tense I felt and how narrow my mind had become, I remembered that Alice is right—the antidote to this deep dread is to relax and surrender to what I can't control—life itself.

> You might think that worry is a useful thing to do during a crisis, but a mind filled with catastrophic possibilities is not helpful at all. When you notice negative obsessive and repetitive thoughts, it's time to move your attention out of your head and into your body. Sit down and put your hands on your belly and take five deep breaths. Take a walk or a shower. Exercise. If you're in bed, get up and drink some hot tea or stretch.

Any crisis forces you to face a truth that you likely forget in your "regular" life—that you and all you love are vulnerable to danger and disease and have little control over events. Even if you do all the "right" things—not engaging in risky behavior like drinking, reckless driving, or eating an unhealthy diet—you're still at risk. Tom thought of this when his ten-year-old son lay unconscious in the intensive care unit after a fall from his skateboard. Tom kept thinking, "But he was wearing a helmet," as though that made his son immune to terrible injury. But when his family's pastor came to pray with him and his wife, he reminded Tom that the same rain falls on both the just and the unjust, gently telling him that no one—including his son—is free from the laws of nature, no matter how cherished, virtuous, or loved they might be.

You can—and should—do your best to keep everyone safe in difficult times, but also remember that it's not always in your power to guarantee safety. If you find yourself caught in a terrible dread of all the awful things that could happen, I encourage you to notice your body and go for a walk or do deep breathing exercises to alleviate your tension and relax into the moment. You can also try "Giving It Up to the Universe," which has helped me throughout my life to surrender to what is and relax into the mystery of being human. Even though I'm a skeptical agnostic and don't worship a God, I do know that when I "give it up to the universe"—let go of my attempts to control the uncontrollable—I feel great relief and clarity and when I connect with the poignant impermanent circumstances of all living beings, I feel deep compassion for everyone, including myself. "Giving It Up to the Universe" is not a prayer to ask a divine being to intercede on your behalf, but rather an offering to help you acknowledge your limitations, relax, and let go of what you can't change or fix. So whatever your beliefs— even if you're an atheist materialist—I invite you to learn to relax the next time you're experiencing the deep and painful sense of dread.

Apranihita is a Sanskrit word that translates as "aimlessness" or "wishlessness"—a state of experiencing exactly what's happening in the present moment without leaning forward. It's hard to do because nearly all of us in life and in meditation have some kind of aim or goal—what Zen teachers call a "gaining idea." With meditation students, the goal is often to become a "better" person or to make the breath deeper or to stop thoughts from chattering. Having a gaining idea prevents us from relaxing into right now and disconnects us from the present. If we have an aim or a goal, it compromises our ability to be with the future too, because we're looking ahead into the distance and not letting the next moment arise as it is. You can tell if you have a gaining idea when you feel disappointed or let down with who you are or with your meditation practice. This disappointment is an insightful opportunity to notice that you're looking for something, to stop looking, and to be here now with *apranihita*.

Practice 10: Giving It Up to the Universe

You don't have to be a religious person to understand that life is a great mystery and the events of the world are not in our power. If you rage against a natural disaster, a health crisis, an accident, or any other terrible situation, you will cause yourself more suffering on top of the suffering you're already experiencing. And if you're filled with dread, allowing your mind to generate more and more fatalistic fears and worries, you're adding to the difficulties of an already anxious situation. This practice will let you acknowledge your limitations and give your concerns to something greater than yourself. Whether you believe in such a thing or not doesn't matter—what matters is that you're letting go of what you can't control and giving yourself a chance to relax, to stop trying to fix or figure out something that is not up to you at all.

1. Find a quiet spot where you won't be disturbed.

2. Bring your attention to your breath, breathe deeply, and put your hand on your heart or your belly where you can feel your body move with every inhalation and exhalation. Notice what is happening—scary thoughts, shallow breathing, tightness in your chest. Whatever it is, silently say "yes" to it.

3. Now imagine you're in touch with a powerful force. For you this might be the God or Jesus or Allah of the Judeo-Christian-Islamic religions, Buddhist deities like Quan Yin, Hindu gods like Shiva, or deities from other traditions. You can also connect with what recovery groups call a "higher power"—something beyond yourself that represents everything that is unknown and all that is out of our control. I like to think of this higher

power as the universe. For me, the universe represents the great mystery of life and death, and it is the force or presence or spark that connects all living beings.

4. Keep your hand on your heart and feel your feet on the ground. As you exhale, rest into this powerful force with a sigh of letting go—of your ideas, plans, and strategies. Allow your shoulders to drop and relax your jaw and other places that might be tense as you release whatever negative outcome you're clutching tightly.

5. Finally, give up and let go of your concerns, your dread, your terror, to this powerful force. I say something to myself like, "Universe, I give it all up to you. I relinquish all my fears and terrors and put them in your hands. I surrender to life as it is. Please guide my actions with compassion and wisdom." You can give it up to your powerful force with whatever words or images are appropriate for you.

6. You can repeat this last step as needed, exhaling and letting go and surrendering, whenever and wherever you feel helpless and afraid.

7. Before you conclude this meditation, take a moment to deeply inhale and fully exhale a few times and then thank yourself and your powerful force—whether you believe in it or not.

CHAPTER 11

When You Need Help

"What is the bravest thing you've ever said?" asked the boy.

"Help," said the horse.

"Asking for help isn't giving up," said the horse. "It's refusing to give up."

—CHARLIE MACKESY[1]

LOTS OF PEOPLE NEED HELP IN A CRISIS, AND YOU MIGHT BE ONE OF them. If your home is damaged or destroyed, you might need a place to live, money to pay for repairs or replacing furniture and clothing, and food. If your family member had a sudden stroke and you're spending all your time at their bedside at the hospital, you might need people to pick up your kids from school, feed your pets, or even clean your house. Any unexpected distressing event can cause depression, post-traumatic stress disorder, anxiety attacks, or other mental and emotional difficulties, so you might need to talk to a mental health professional or a spiritual counselor—or at least a caring friend with whom you can share your concerns.

If you think you're supposed to be independent and self-reliant and do everything for yourself, you're wrong! Every day, all of us count on others for love and care, food, electricity, health care, employment, emergency services, and so much more. Take a minute to consider all the help you've received just in the past twenty-four hours to remind yourself that you need other people, like it or not.

You might be ashamed or embarrassed to ask for help because you think you should be able to handle this situation on your own, or you might pride yourself on being self-sufficient and unable to admit that you need support, or maybe you associate accepting help with being weak and vulnerable, like Amba, my friend's new neighbor in Kingston. After she was diagnosed with lupus, Amba became immune compromised, and during cold and flu season in winter, she was afraid to leave her home for fear of exposure to germs and viruses. Most of her friends and family lived in Boston, which was too far away for them to help much. She needed local help getting groceries and medications. She considered leaving a note for a neighbor but was embarrassed to ask a stranger. After her mom reminded her that all the families on their block in Boston did favors for each other all the time, Amba decided she would ask her neighbors. She put on a face mask to protect herself from germs and talked to the woman next door, who was gracious and kind. For the next few months, she picked up what Amba needed and left the bags at her door.

We all rely on help from others all the time, and although you might not like to admit it, you've been supported by others throughout your life. As a child you were cared for by family, teachers, neighbors, friends, medical professionals, and even strangers. Now that you're an adult, each moment of your life continues to be dependent on the efforts of so many others—your electricity is provided by everyone who works at your utility company, your food is cultivated by farm workers and brought to your local store by truck drivers, and simple necessities such as toothpaste, shampoo, and bed linens are made, shipped, and distributed thanks to the work of countless unseen people. This is called *interdependence* in the Buddhist tradition—the fact of our reciprocal, interconnected, relational lives. Interdependence is the opposite of what many of us have learned—that we should be independent, self-sufficient, entirely autonomous—but that is truly impossible.

A decade ago I attended a lecture on interdependence given by the Tibetan teacher Ponlop Rinpoche. He told us that decades before, when he came to the United States to attend college, he was puzzled because so many of his fellow students proudly described themselves as "independent." In Rinpoche's upbringing and training, there was no such thing as "independent," so he wondered if maybe these students were farmers. We all laughed, and you might be laughing too, because independence is such a common misperception. But it's causing harm to so many of us, because the truth is that we all need each other, and when we resist this, we suffer. If you take any kind of medication, even aspirin, then you are dependent on others. If you wear manufactured clothing or shoes, then you're dependent on others. If you have equipment that runs on fuel—gasoline or diesel—then you are dependent on others. Even those living "off the grid" are dependent on others to enforce laws, manufacture machinery parts, and provide food items that they can't grow, like coffee, chocolate, or wine. And businesses that claim to be self-sufficient actually depend upon public infrastructure and services like roads, bridges, electricity, police, and fire departments.

Knowing the truth of interdependence is the deepest wisdom you can cultivate because when you understand how much our lives depend on each other, you recognize that your actions affect so many and so many others affect you. Then you're not ashamed to ask for help or annoyed to give help. Briana said as much after her teenaged son had a mental health crisis, locking himself in a school bathroom and threatening to take his own life. She said to me, "Why is 'dependent' a dirty word? My son needs support, care, and guidance from his family, his teachers, and counselors, and there's nothing wrong with it—we're all dependent on each other and I want him to know he shouldn't feel ashamed—nobody should." It's this wisdom that will guide you to ask for what you need and receive it with gratitude.

Don't be afraid to use all your resources: ask the stranger who lives upstairs to check your mail while you're taking care of your sick mother; apply for state and federal loans, private grants, and other possible benefits if you're eligible; contact organizations in your network; make an appointment with a therapist to discuss your emotional state. It takes courage to allow yourself to be vulnerable, to focus on your health and well-being, and to remember that life is constantly changing—right now you might need to receive, but you'll have opportunities to give too.

Interdependence, sometimes called interbeing, means mutual support and connection—that what you do affects yourself and others too. In an old Buddhist teaching, the *Sedaka Sutta*,[2] the Buddha talks to two circus performers. For their act, a woman stood on a man's shoulders as he walked across a tightrope high above the ground. The woman told the Buddha that they each have to be mindful of themselves so that they don't cause one another harm. This dependency on each other for safety is a metaphor for all of us. It tells us that if we care for ourselves wisely—with mindfulness, compassion, and kindness—we're also caring for others and the safety of the world around us. At the end of the *sutta*, the Buddha praises their wisdom, saying, "Looking after yourself, you look after others; and looking after others, you look after yourself."

Practice 11: Giving and Receiving

When a fire destroyed more than a dozen apartments in a nearby building, my neighbors and I collected donations and contributed clothing and furniture, and when Lori's brother Scott slipped while putting salt down in his Milwaukee driveway in January, she rushed to the hospital to be with him, happy that he relied on her enough to call her. You've probably given to others like this countless times, and remembering this will help you feel more open to receiving from others when you're in need. This meditation helps you connect to the reality of all that you give and receive.

1. Find a quiet spot, put away your devices, close your eyes, and inhale and exhale slowly and deeply five times.

2. Recall an occasion when someone helped you out—a friend recommended you for a job, a teacher tutored you, a neighbor picked up your kids from day care, a family member lent you money or gave you a place to stay—and silently say "thank you."

3. Let yourself remember a few more of these situations. They could be great gestures of support, such as a time when someone loaned you a large sum of money, or small gestures, like the time when someone held the elevator for you when you were late to work or noticed your scarf left behind on the bus and returned it to you.

4. Take a few conscious breaths, and now let yourself remember a time when you helped someone out. The time that you recommended a friend for a job, tutored someone, listened to a family member who was upset, took food to a neighbor after their mom died—and silently say "thank you" to yourself.

5. Think of a few more of these situations when you were generous and kind. They could be big gestures, such as loaning someone a large sum of money, or small gestures, like holding the elevator for someone who was late to work or noticing the child who dropped their mittens in the drugstore. Again, silently say "thank you" to yourself.

6. Finally, put your hand on your heart and silently say, "May I give and receive easily. May we all give and receive easily." Stay quiet and still for a few minutes, and before you get up, be sure to appreciate yourself by saying "thank you."

CHAPTER 12

When You're Mad at the World

What if the way we respond to our problems is part of the problem?
—BAYO AKOMOLAFE[1]

RECENTLY, I WOKE UP ONE MORNING FEELING OUTRAGED AND FRUS-
trated with the entire world. I'd watched hours of cable news reports
on the latest global crisis before bed. I fumed in the kitchen as I made
coffee, thinking about how stupid human beings are and how we're
destroying each other and the planet. As my husband reached into
the cabinet above my head for the Cheerios, he noticed me talking to
myself. "What's wrong?" he asked.

"It's all wrong!" I yelled and burst into tears.

I cried because beneath my anger was such sadness and sorrow for everyone who is suffering and will continue to suffer due
to human ignorance and inaction and the resulting and ongoing
catastrophes that we see and read about every day: armed conflict
and violence across the globe, hungry polar bears without ice on
which to live or hunt, ongoing racism, sexism, and oppression right
here in the United States.

You might feel similarly right now, reading and watching the
media where you witness so much destruction and human ignorance
and selfishness. Like me, maybe you've been trying to hide your sadness under anger or indifference, hoping it would protect you from

having to feel your grief at so much needless suffering. However, I encourage you to let your heart break for the world, to feel your tender concern and sadness, and to let your natural compassion arise. If you continue to resist these vulnerable and beautiful feelings, your heart will stay closed—to yourself and the world too. Your anger will prevent you from sharing your compassion and wisdom when it's needed the most.

> If you're enraged—feeling overwhelmed with hostility, aggression, or hatred, take a breath. Even if you feel that your rage is justified, it's causing you harm and clouding your ability to make wise decisions for yourself and others. Put your hand on your heart and breathe in your rage and breathe out your patience until you feel steadier.

After the 2016 election, certain students and friends angrily said to me, "I hate Donald Trump." Because I'm a meditation teacher and a Buddhist, they expressed it with defiance or shame, expecting me to chastise them and tell them to be more loving or to admonish them and tell them they're wrong to hate. Instead, I told them, "Your hatred isn't bothering Donald Trump. It's bothering you."

It's not morally wrong and you're not a bad person for feeling hatred, hostility, or anger toward someone who is dangerous, violent, and/or causing harm or toward a situation that is obviously destructive. But I can assure you that your hatred is likely not affecting your enemies at all—although it's probably upsetting you and those closest to you. It's making you physically tense or even sick, it's obscuring your ability to see clearly and act wisely, and it won't bring about any positive change to the situation or the world. Even (or especially) a soldier fighting a just war can do so more effectively without a heart filled with hatred.

Though emotions like hatred or hostility make you feel powerful and strong, the world doesn't need more hatred or hostility. What the world desperately needs is for you to develop and share your good qualities with yourself and others. This is the appropriate response to the world's suffering and pain—cultivating the compassion, love, and caring necessary to alleviate it and to create conditions for all living beings to flourish. This is one of the reasons I wrote this book—not only to help you reduce stress, deal with difficult emotions, and care for yourself and your loved ones during painful times, but also to enable you to recognize the value of your gifts: your deep wisdom, compassion, and courage. When expressed through your words, actions, and presence, your gifts can contribute to creating a healthy and equitable world for everyone. I was able to offer my greatest gifts—love, wisdom, understanding, and joy—only when I let my heart break. When I truly felt the terribleness of what is happening in our world, I was able to give, without hatred, to all who need it. And so will you.

In Buddhism, a *paritta* is a teaching, chant, or verse that is repeatedly spoken aloud and believed to provide safety, health, and happiness to a person or community. *Paritta* means protection or safeguard, and you can protect your mind against the poisons of hatred, greed, and delusion by cultivating truth, virtue, and love by reciting protection chants. One of the most beloved Buddhist *parittas* is the "*Karaniya Metta Sutta*: The Hymn of Universal Love."[2] Two of its most beautiful passages follow, and I hope you'll read them aloud three times to yourself. Do this several times today and notice how saying these words aloud connects you to your heart and deepens your wisdom.

Verse 7

Mata yatha niyam puttam	Just as with her own life
Ayusa ekaputtam anurakkhe	A mother shields her child, her only child, from hurt
Evampi sabbabhutesu	Let all-embracing thoughts
Manasam bhavaye aparimanam	For all beings be yours.

Verse 8

Mettañ ca sabba-lokasmim	Cultivate a limitless heart of goodwill
Manasam bhavaye aparimanam	For all throughout the cosmos,
Uddham adho ca tiriyanca	In all its height, depth and breadth—
Asambadham averam asapattam	Love that is untroubled and beyond hatred or enmity.

Practice 12: Letting Your Heart Break

The last thing most of us want to do is to feel all the suffering there is in the world—it's heartbreaking in its immensity and extent. Yet our nature as human beings is to make connections with others, to reach out our hand during times of need, and to offer compassion to those who struggle with sorrow, pain, and crisis. You can remember and restore your nature by paying attention to your thoughts and feelings and sharing your inherent capacity for caring with yourself. Then you can expand it to include your closest family and friends, your community, strangers, enemies, and all living beings, all of us linked through this experience of life itself.

1. Find a quiet place to sit down for a bit and shut off your phone, computer, and television. If you're at home, ask the people you live with to leave you undisturbed for ten minutes. If you're at work, take a seat in the break room; if you're at the office, find an empty conference room.

2. Don't do anything for a minute or two. Just sit there and be still.

3. Place your attention on your belly, feeling it move as you inhale and exhale. Take a moment to follow your breath.

4. Now put your hand on your heart and quietly say to yourself, *I'm here for you, and it's okay to be upset.* Repeat silently with kindness, as though you're speaking to someone you love very much.

5. After a few minutes, imagine someone you know who might also be feeling the way you feel or who is struggling or upset and say to them silently, *May you be free from suffering and be at peace.*

6. Finally, consider everyone everywhere who are in crisis, pain, or sorrow, and give this same kindness and wisdom to all by repeating silently: *May we all be free from suffering and be at peace.*

7. Before you conclude this contemplation, take a few moments to sit quietly without doing or saying anything. Then say thank you to yourself.

CHAPTER 13

What to Do When You're Afraid

The difference between fear and harmony is how you handle your thoughts.

—TSOKNYI RINPOCHE[1]

IF YOU'RE IN DANGER OF BEING ATTACKED BY A LION, THEN FEAR IS necessary and useful. It's telling you to get yourself out of an unsafe situation—*fast*. But other times it's neither necessary nor useful and it overwhelms your ability to see what's happening in reality. Right now, you might be afraid—it's a natural response to a crisis. But you want to be sure that your fear is appropriate and respond to it compassionately, or its power and energy can mislead you and cause you to panic, act recklessly, or make bad decisions.

Cassie learned this when she and her husband Lee decided to stay in their home in Asbury Park during Hurricane Sandy. Although they were told to evacuate by the authorities, they had lots of food and water and a generator, so they felt confident they could weather the storm safely. But when part of the roof was swept away exposing the kitchen ceiling to the rain, Cassie looked at her one-year-old daughter and felt like a fool. She became so terrified that she insisted to her husband that they leave immediately, even though the governor had warned everyone to stay in place after the storm began. They packed up their car, backed out of the garage, but didn't get much past their driveway before realizing the streets around their home were impassable and there were downed power lines everywhere. Her husband said, "Cassie, I know you're afraid but you have to stop panicking. We need to go back home and ride this out." She cried and hugged the baby, and although she was shaking with fear, she knew he was right. They went back, sheltered in their upstairs bedroom overnight with blankets and a crank radio, and when the storm receded the next morning, the downstairs of their house was flooded but they were safe.

> If you're filled with fear, take a deep breath, stop, and get quiet for a moment. Are you in immediate danger? If so, act mindfully and carefully to get yourself and your family to safety as quickly as you can. If you're not, put your hand on your heart and say, "Fear is in me and it's okay."

When you feel afraid, use mindfulness to pause and sense what's happening in your body and mind. Don't act impulsively, like Cassie. If you're able to notice that you're afraid, you can prevent fear from escalating into desperation, anger, or ignorance—the three poisonous mind-states that obscure your good sense. Notice how your body feels to help you understand the reality of your situation and to slow down your reactions. Use your senses to truly comprehend what's happening in your environment—what you can see and hear. Then you can gain clarity about what you need to do—or not do. I learned this after years of being a fearful flyer. Every time I was on an airplane and felt turbulence, I thought it was about to crash. I stared at the flight attendants and imagined they showed signs of concern, thought I saw problems with the wings and the engines through the windows, and even imagined I smelled smoke. Sometimes I asked people around me if they noticed a problem (they didn't). But now I've learned to mindfully pay attention to my environment and notice that there is no problem with the plane. The problem is that I'm experiencing fear, even terror. During a flight—or anytime I feel afraid for no reason, like when I'm home alone at night and think I hear a noise outside—I put my hand on my heart, take a deep breath, and say to myself out loud, "Fear is arising." I say it a few times because it's the truth, and it brings me back to the reality of my situation: fear is happening in me; all the other things that I think are happening outside of me are not. When I understand that there is no threat coming at me, there's nothing for me to do except to take care of myself and my emotions with patience and concentration. I breathe regularly and deeply, reassure myself that I'm safe, and calm down.

The next time you're afraid, take time to get clear on what's really happening before taking any action. Use mindfulness practice to bring your attention to your senses, not just your thoughts, and give yourself time to consider your choices and the possible outcomes of your decisions before saying or doing anything.

Buddhist contemplative techniques are designed to help us see our own minds—our mental images, thoughts, and feelings. They help us see how the internal habits, emotions, and reactions of our mind can distort our perception of external events. The following is an old story called "The Snake" that likely predates Buddhism, but I've heard it from many teachers, and it's a great example of how common and powerful misperceptions can be.

A woman, walking alone through a dense forest, sees a large tree has fallen across the path, blocking the way ahead of her. She can't go around the tree because the ground beyond the path is flooded and muddy. She pauses to consider if she can climb over it, then sees a large poisonous snake coiled on top of the tree trunk. She gasps, steps back in fear, and nearly turns to run, but when she glances again, she isn't quite sure that she sees a snake. As she looks more carefully, she realizes that it's actually an old piece of rope, probably left behind by loggers in the area. She sighs, scrambles over the top of the log, and resumes her walk.

Practice 13: Facing Fear

Fear activates physical sensations that are out of your control, like increased heart rate and shallow respiration, and might cause you to feel as if you should run or freeze. You can't switch off these physical sensations, but you don't have to be overwhelmed by them or react to them unless it's necessary. This practice will help you learn to notice them and slow down to give yourself the space and time needed to choose what to do instead of simply reacting. I've relied on the following meditation many times when I've been afraid, and it enables me to bring attention to my racing thoughts and feel less overwhelmed, and it will help you too.

1. Wherever you are—you could be in a car, in your living room watching television, or on an airplane—start by recognizing your fear. Too often we don't even know or want to acknowledge that we're afraid, because we're more worried about what's going on outside of us than inside. Recognizing fear means sensing your body and emotions and seeing that fear is here. Then stop for a moment, put your hand on your heart, and say to yourself, "Fear is arising."

2. Next, turn off all your devices, close your book, and get still. If you're at home, lie down flat if that's possible (without using a pillow or slouching on the couch), preferably somewhere comfortable, such as on your bed or the floor. Now feel the weight of your body on the Earth and invite yourself to relax.

3. You can close your eyes or keep them open, whatever is most steadying for your mind as you take a moment to notice where fear is arising. Is it in your belly? Are your palms sweaty or is

your heart racing? What kind of thoughts are coming up? Pay attention to physical sensations with patience and curiosity. If you get caught up in the fearful thoughts, put your hand on your heart and say, "Fear is arising" again and return to your body.

4. Now rest one hand on your heart and one hand on your belly, and count nine breaths, feeling the rise of your body through your palms. Each full sequence counts for one breath—inhale/ exhale one . . . inhale/exhale two . . . continuing until you get to nine full breaths, then start over at one.

5. If you get mixed up and miss a breath or get caught up in ideas, images, or thoughts, it's okay. Just start again at one, as many times as needed. Continue this practice for at least ten minutes or until your breath is regulated—it sometimes takes me up to thirty minutes to relax. Repeat as necessary.

CHAPTER 14

When Others Behave Badly

If you think you're enlightened, spend a week with your family.
—RAM DASS[1]

MY FATHER WAS A DIFFICULT MAN, AND EVEN WHEN HE WAS eighty-nine years old, he was determined to do what he wanted, when he wanted, no matter if it wasn't in his best interest or it could even be harmful to himself or others. It wasn't a surprise that he refused to stop driving, even after a serious accident in which he lost control of his car, hit a guardrail, careened across two lanes of traffic, and wound up stuck on the median. Although his neighbors and friends volunteered to take him wherever he needed so he wouldn't have to drive, he rejected them, insisting that he was perfectly capable of driving. I tried demanding, cajoling, and yelling to prevent him from driving, but he stubbornly insisted that he wasn't worried and I shouldn't be either, that I should leave him alone about it, and refused to talk about it again.

Right now, you might be concerned or frustrated about the behavior of others too. They might be family members and friends or even strangers or world leaders. You may be feeling so worried that you're insisting or nagging or demanding that they do what you want, and when they don't, you're angry or annoyed with them. Although it's natural to care about others and want everyone to be safe and healthy, the truth is, it's unnatural to believe that we can make anyone do what we want them to do. There are many people who, like my father, for one reason or another, won't listen, prepare, or take the proper precautions to stay safe or healthy, and sometimes they even cause a crisis. They might even act in ways that endanger others as well as themselves, like Terrence and Lydia's neighbor Pete, who refused to shovel and salt the sidewalk in front of his big Chicago bungalow, even during the worst blizzard of the season. Lydia volunteered to spread salt on it herself but Pete refused, even after she threatened to call their alderman. Terrence watched from the living room window as the wind roared and worried for his neighbors on their way to and from the grocery store on the corner for supplies. He winced as an elderly lady cautiously tiptoed in her snow boots over the solid, uneven ice patch in front of Pete's bungalow.

> If you're so mad at another person's bad behavior that you're ready to yell, insult, or physically hit or throw something at them, that's a sign to sit down and take a deep breath. Trying to control another person is like hitting your head against the wall—it only injures you and does little harm to the wall. Instead, put your hand on your heart and repeat to yourself as you breathe, "Everything is not up to me."

There seems to always be that one person who makes a crisis *worse*. The guy who wants to take his guns to peaceful protests or the woman yelling at her father's surgeon and telling her how to do her job. There's my cousin's dad, a retired schoolteacher in the Midwest who warns against the "New World Order"—an elite cabal of billionaires who are creating a shadow government that will control the world—on seemingly every Facebook post following a mass shooting. I and other family members have taken the time to explain to him that he's wrong and link him to information that explains this fake news, but he won't listen or believe us. Like my father and Terrence and Lydia's neighbor Pete, it's impossible to make him do what I want him to do, so I delete his comments and ignore most of his posts.

During a crisis or not, we all want others to act with consideration, caring, and respect, and sometimes we struggle with what to say to them. Who hasn't unsuccessfully attempted to explain to a friend why they're wrong or prevent their kids or spouse from making a bad decision or warn someone about the dangers of drinking, abusing drugs, staying in a toxic relationship, or dropping out of college? At best, your advice is ignored, and at worst, it offends or upsets the person you care about, straining your relationship.

Trying to control what we can't control is a common source of unnecessary confusion and pain. We know we can't control other people—or the weather, growing older, or getting sick—but that doesn't stop us from trying. In the Buddhist tradition, recognizing the limits of what we can control is a form of wisdom called *uphek-kha*—equanimity. Equanimity is a quality that enables us to let go of demands and expectations so that we can keep a steady mind and a kind heart no matter the circumstances. Developing equanimity enables us to say yes to what's outside of our control, even when we don't like what's happening or what someone is doing. It allows us to continue to love and care for someone, even as we discern that their actions may hurt themselves or others.

You can certainly offer your support, guidance, and suggestions to the people in your life, but if they're refused or ignored, equanimity helps you to let go of your attachment to being "right." It helps you understand that you can't predict the future and don't know for sure what is going to happen. Although I worried about my father as he continued to drive, equanimity allowed me to accept that I didn't know if he would get in an accident and that I had to stop nagging and let him do what he wanted to do for my own peace of mind. And although I'm angry about the stupidity of the Facebook posts by my cousin's dad, equanimity reminds me that I can't make him change his mind or his ignorance.

So if you find yourself frustrated or annoyed that people in your life—those close to you or not—are not doing what you think they should do during a crisis, it's time to consider letting go of your wishes and advice and instead remind yourself that not everything is up to you and that you can't change other people—but you can change yourself.

Sometimes people think that Buddhists don't "take sides" or that we think that whatever happens is "okay." But the opposite is true. Having a sense of balance and equanimity is not the same as a lack of discernment or judgment. The entire Buddhist training path— ethics, contemplation, and wisdom—is designed to develop an understanding of what actions are wholesome, skillful, beneficial, and not harmful, and what actions are not. This includes knowing what is in our control and what is out of our control so that we can wisely focus our attention on what we *can* do. And knowing that we can't control someone else but also seeing that their actions are dangerous doesn't mean we do nothing—it means we do whatever we can to stop them from doing harm.

Practice 14: Letting Go

Other people rank highly on most of our lists as the cause of many of our deepest difficulties and frustrations. When they behave badly—especially in a crisis—we might find ourselves enraged, angry, or even in pain. We might think that if they really cared about us, they would behave differently, or if they were the "good" people that they think they are, then they would act with better judgment. But the truth is that everyone does the best they can do, and if they could do better, they would. When we try to change other people, we really suffer, so if you're caught in a moment of upset with someone else, try this practice. Remember, it's not for them, but for you.

1. Find a quiet spot, get still, put your hand on your heart, and take a few deep breaths. Be sure to shut off all your devices and ask your family or roommates to leave you alone for a while. Sit up straight in a comfortable chair.

2. Close your eyes and imagine the person who is frustrating you. You can imagine them as you know them, or see them as a child, or just feel their presence with you. When you've connected with them, say to them silently, *I release you from my demands and expectations of you.* Continue repeating this silently to them. You might get caught in anger or a story about how awful they're acting and get swept away from this practice. That's okay. Just notice what's happening and choose to begin again. Reconnect with this person and start over, repeating silently, *I release you from my demands and expectations of you.*

3. Now imagine you and the frustrating person together. You can imagine you're looking in each other's eyes or that they are

sitting near you and silently say, *May we be peaceful and happy.* Repeat this silently as if you're giving both of you a gift. You might feel agitated or annoyed or resistant to saying this. You might think they don't deserve this. It's okay. Just notice your thoughts and choose to come back and start again, repeating this blessing.

4. After ten minutes or so, you can stop saying the phrases and imagining the other person. Just let yourself feel your body and your heart, and welcome whatever you're feeling with kindness. When you're ready, you can conclude the practice by thanking yourself for your willingness to release and let go.

CHAPTER 15

When You're Restless and Bored

To realize that boredom does not come from the object of our attention but rather from the quality of our attention is truly a transforming insight.

—JOSEPH GOLDSTEIN[1]

AT THE START, ALL CRISES ARE ACUTE AND IMMEDIATE, AND WE have to attend to them quickly—we have no choice. But when the acute phase is over, you could be facing a longer, less critical, but still exhausting and troubling time. You or someone you love could be facing a long decline into debilitating old age, recovery from illness or trauma, or months of rebuilding or cleaning up after a storm or fire. At this point, you might think that your days are monotonous and dull, and you're bored and uninterested.

That's how Lawrence felt soon after his ninety-five-year-old mom fell. She lived alone for years and refused to move in with her children or even let them get her assistance. When they phoned her the week after Christmas and she didn't answer, his sister, who lived nearby, found her on the bathroom floor and called an ambulance. She had a serious urinary tract infection and spent nearly two weeks in the hospital. They wouldn't let her go home alone, so Lawrence—divorced and able to do some of his work remotely—said he would stay with her temporarily. But four months passed, and although he technically didn't live there, he only slept at his own house on Friday and Saturday, when his sister and brother and their kids visited his mom. She wasn't expected to fully recover, spent most of her time in bed, and would likely need help caring for herself for the rest of her life. Lawrence hated this boring new routine and how it limited his life but also felt guilty for feeling this way about his beloved mother.

> If you feel you're tired of waiting for something to be over, *stop*. The truth is that you're living your life right now, even if it's not the way you want it or you know it's temporary. Close your eyes, put your hand on your heart, feel your feet on the ground, and say to yourself, "I'm here and now." Repeat this reminder often.

The antidote for boredom or tedium is to pay closer attention. Because even if we follow the same day-to-day routine, if we look closely, we can see that it's all changing all the time—the weather fluctuates, our moods vary, and we can't reliably predict what people around us will say or do. With curiosity and practice, we can use mindfulness to notice what's happening and transform our boredom into interest. That's what happens in *Groundhog Day*, one of my favorite movies. Bill Murray plays a man visiting Punxsutawney, Pennsylvania, for the annual Groundhog Day holiday. He's planning to stay overnight at a local hotel and return to New York the next day, but when he wakes up the next morning, it's Groundhog Day again—and it's exactly the same as the day before. This continues day after day, and he ultimately realizes he's stuck in the same time and place. At first, he hates it and tries everything to make it end—attempting to destroy himself in car crashes and suicides, trying to kill the groundhog and ruin the festival, treating everyone he encounters with meanness, contempt, and cruelty, but none of it works. Then he figures as long as he's stuck in the same day, he'll exploit it. He manipulates the people around him, seduces the woman he loves, and takes whatever he wants—expensive clothing, jewelry, wine—knowing he'll never get caught. After that, he's so bored that nothing interests him. He drinks, does drugs, stays in bed all day, pays no attention to what's happening, and feels that nothing he does matters because tomorrow he'll wake up and it will be the same day all over again. But finally, after a long, long time—perhaps centuries—he burns through his hatred, greed, and boredom. He stops trying to change events and instead starts to pay attention—to be mindful of the present moment. Each morning he wakes up and responds with unthinking compassion and wisdom to whatever and whomever he encounters, and when he does this, he's happy and free.

You can take inspiration from Bill Murray and learn to pay attention to what's happening in this very moment too. That's what Lawrence did. He took a mindfulness-based stress reduction class, and suddenly he saw things he'd overlooked—he noticed the family photos in his bedroom and asked his mom about the people in them. One morning he saw there were buds on the cherry tree outside the back window and it delighted him, because just a week earlier, the branches were bare. And now he actually heard the kids playing next door, and it made him smile. As he took greater notice and interest in the world around him, he felt less bored and more connected—to himself and everyone else.

If you feel stuck or restless or bored, like you've seen it all already, try to remember that you haven't. Each moment is brand new and has never happened before and never will again, and if you don't pay attention, you'll miss it. Use mindfulness to focus on your senses—feel the air on your skin, hear the sounds entering your ears and your breath. The more you look, the more you'll see—and you'll soon discover that there's so much more going on than you ever imagined.

We might not recognize it, but boredom is a type of *dukkha*—a suffering and dissatisfaction with the present moment. It's caused by *tanha*, which is usually translated as craving but literally means thirst—a desperate desire for something else to be happening other than what actually *is* happening. Craving leads us to mindlessly binge-watch television or have a glass of wine when we're bored. The antidote to it is recognizing *dukkha* with kindness and compassion and noticing that it's not being caused by anything outside of us but rather by our own *tanha*. Then by practicing mindfulness of our body sensations, with gentleness and care, our energy and interest increase and our craving—*tanha*—dissolves.

Practice 15: Looking Closer

Most of us don't want to experience boredom, monotony, or tedium—when they arise in us, we want to feel something else. But just as the opposite of boredom is interest, it's also its antidote. Taking an interest in what's actually happening during times of dullness or restlessness means that we look more closely—sharpen our attention to actually experience our mind and sensations. When we do this, we can see that what we call boredom is really only a lack of awareness, easily dispelled by fully engaging with the moment.

1. Ask the people you live with to leave you undisturbed, turn off your computer and television, and find a seat near a window (open, if weather permits). Set a timer on your phone for ten minutes, then set the phone more than an arm's reach away from you.

2. Sit comfortably with your feet on the floor and don't move around.

3. Keep your eyes open but still, and let your gaze fall gently to the floor. Just allow the light to enter your eyes. Don't look out the window or search for something to see.

4. Notice that you're breathing—feel your inhalations and your exhalations without trying to change them as you allow your body to breathe naturally.

5. Gently bring your attention to your ears. Pay attention to sounds entering from indoors and outdoors, sounds of birds or cars, the sound of your own breath or heartbeat. You don't have to push any of them away or try to hear them better. You don't

have to do anything at all—you're not "listening," rather you're allowing the sounds to come to you.

6. If you get distracted by thoughts of what you're going to do later or memories, images, or conversations, gently return your attention to sounds. Receive them all—close, near, pleasant, unpleasant, boring.

7. If you find yourself overwhelmed and you want to get up, bring your attention back to your breath by putting your hand on your stomach and feeling it rise and fall with your respiration. Deeply exhale—sigh—several times. Then return to noticing sounds enter your ears.

8. When the timer rings, shut it off then pause for a moment. Stay still and thank yourself for your effort.

9. Try to do this practice for at least ten minutes twice a day. You'll be able to notice the changes by sitting at the window at different times, and your natural curiosity and interest will arise as you look and listen more closely at the world around you.

CHAPTER 16

A Crisis of Faith

There are infinite numbers of Buddhas and infinite numbers of beings. Who can say who is excluded from it?
—NYOSHUL KHEN RINPOCHE[1]

MY FRIEND JEWEL WORKS AT A NEW YORK CITY HIGH SCHOOL, AND they love their job. But after a shooting in a church in their hometown in Texas, where nearly a dozen people were killed or injured, they texted me and said, "I am having a hard time believing in the goodness of people recently. Even with all my beautiful students."

Like Jewel, maybe you've lost faith in humanity, or you struggle to find common ground or shared values with friends and family. Watching the news or social media, you might think everyone is an idiot or that human beings are terrible because of all the destruction, hatred, and stupidity we cause. It can be really hard to believe in people when everything seems to be falling apart, but you don't have to believe in everyone—you just need to believe in yourself. When you can remember and notice all of your beautiful qualities, you'll be able to recognize them in others and renew your faith in humanity and the world.

A fundamental principle of Buddhism is *tathāgatagarbha*—buddha nature. Buddha nature means having the nature of a buddha, which is clear, wise, and compassionate. Each of us—every human being—is born with buddha nature. We're all buddhas—we just don't know it yet. We don't see our buddha nature, sometimes called our true nature, clearly or understand our innate potential because our mind is obscured by our habits and conditioning and our neediness, aversions, and confusions. Unlike some religion traditions that believe that humans are born flawed or some psychological views that believe people are innately violent and aggressive, Buddhism exposes the truth of our lives and our nature—that we are born loving, joyful, and wise. Brain scientists have recently begun to confirm this truth—qualities like compassion are inherent in human beings and simply need to be fostered by our environment to develop.[2]

When you feel cynicism, contempt, or scorn for someone else's opinion—in real life with a family member or on the internet with a stranger—stop and pause. Notice how you might have turned this other person into an object, and take a breath, reconnect with your wise qualities, and say to yourself, "This is a feeling human being just like me."

Buddhism is a path to discovering your true nature, and it includes practicing meditation, training in ethical behavior, and cultivating wisdom. When you practice meditation, you develop insight into your suffering, and your deepest intentions to connect, share, love, and be loved are revealed. When you behave ethically to prevent harm, your empathetic nature is revealed. And when you cultivate wisdom— looking clearly at reality—you see the impermanent nature of every living being and the deep suffering we all share, which uncovers your deepest compassion.

As you follow the path, you see for yourself that you possess these beautiful qualities and begin to have confidence that you have buddha nature. And if you do, then everyone else does too. Your cynicism and skepticism will fade if you pay attention and notice the efforts of your friends and family. You'll see that neighbors and strangers want to help and support each other too, and you'll feel more encouraged and optimistic about humanity. Although we sometimes forget to pay attention to good news, we know that we can count on people coming together to support and care for each other in a crisis because it's happened many times. Healthcare workers from all over the country volunteered to travel to New Orleans after Hurricane Katrina, where local restaurants fed hospital workers and displaced people. Nongovernmental organizations from around the world rushed to Haiti when it was devastated by an earthquake, and in most neighborhoods throughout the United States, there are dozens of churches, community groups, and food pantries supporting those in need. If you pay attention, you can see that throughout the world, there are politicians and corporations supporting initiatives to reduce global warming and end racism, and doctors and scientists continue to tirelessly collaborate to discover treatments, vaccines, and cures for disease and human suffering. As you develop your own good heart, you'll recognize the blessings and kindnesses of others and see their goodness and buddha nature too.

You don't have to practice long before gaining the confidence that you have the nature of a buddha. Even if you just sit down quietly right now and remember what you did during the past week, you'll see the kindnesses you naturally offered to yourself and others, and the generosity you frequently shared. You'll also notice your confusion and mistakes—including the times when you've hurt others or taken more than your share. That's because you're not a buddha—yet. Keep practicing with diligence, aspiration, and confidence, and you'll awaken to your full potential and inspire others too.

A Korean Zen teacher explained buddha nature to our class with the following story. I won't explain it because it's up to you to understand its meaning intuitively. Read it a few times and then sit quietly without trying to analyze it or figure it out and see what arises.

A young man wakes up in the morning, looks in the mirror, and doesn't see his head. He hurries down to breakfast with his family and says to his sister desperately, "My head is missing! My head is missing!" She says, "What are you talking about? It's right there!" He runs to his father and says wildly, "Father, my head is missing! Help!" His father looks up from his desk and says, "Your head isn't missing! It's right there!" Finally, he runs to his mother and frantically cries, "Oh my god! My head is missing!" The mother calmly looks at her son and slaps him in the face. The son runs to the mirror, sees his face, touches his stinging cheek, and says with relief, "Oh, here it is. It's been here all along."

Practice 16: Restoring Trust

Sometimes when my husband is reading the news, I overhear him groan or shout in annoyance at someone who said or did something harmful, greedy, or cruel. When I ask him what's wrong, he usually says something like, "I don't even care anymore—I give up!" What he means is that he's discouraged. He's not alone. You might be disheartened or disgusted by the meanness, racism, stupidity, short-sightedness, sexism, or cruelty that you witness from leaders, celebrities, strangers, family, and friends too. The next time you've lost faith in humanity and are ready to give up on all of us, take a moment to practice this exercise to reconnect with and remember the beautiful qualities that we all share.

1. Shut off your computer, phone, or device. Stop talking.

2. Find a quiet spot sitting on a kitchen chair, relaxing on your couch, lying on your bed, sitting in your car, or alone in an office.

3. Set a timer for five minutes and close your eyes.

4. Take several breaths, inhaling slowly and deeply as you imagine you're pulling air through your nose all the way down to your belly.

5. Exhale fully, gently drawing your navel toward your spine.

6. Relax your forehead, cheeks, and jaw while continuing to breathe. Notice the rise and fall of your chest.

7. Bring your attention to the soles of your feet.

8. Notice your impatience, anger, or frustration. Where do you feel this? Is your jaw or chest tight? Do you have images, plans, or

conversations arising in your mind? Whatever is happening is okay; you don't have to get rid of anything. Instead, move your attention back to your body breathing, the rise and fall of your abdomen, the sounds around you.

9. Make a connection with yourself by imagining you're looking in the mirror at yourself. Say to yourself, *May I remember my good heart and wisdom.* Repeat this to yourself for a few minutes.

10. Now think of whoever made you mad. It could be a person or a group of people—Republicans, Progressives, people in Florida or New York, Canada or Russia. Include them in your imagination and say to all of them, *May we remember our good hearts and wisdom.* Repeat.

11. Practice like this until you hear the timer. Then slowly open your eyes, stretch, and say thank you to yourself for connecting to the beautiful qualities you share with all human beings.

CHAPTER 17

Living Alone in a Crisis

*The practice of solitude is the practice of creating an inward auton-
omy within ourselves, an inward freedom from the power of overwhelming thoughts and emotions.*

—STEPHEN BATCHELOR[1]

UNTIL I GOT MARRIED, I'D LIVED ALONE FOR SEVERAL DECADES. I enjoyed my single life in a fifth-floor New York City walk-up. I was a regular at my local coffee shop and laundromat, acquainted with many neighbors, and rarely bored or lonely. I had a network of friends, went to the movies and theater often, and appreciated time by myself to read, cook, or simply take pleasure in silence. Things changed after September 11, 2001, when it wasn't so great to be alone in the aftermath of the attacks. The city was deserted and silent except for the sounds of emergency vehicles, helicopters, and fighter jets, especially in my downtown neighborhood. The cellular cables for the area were cut when the towers fell, so I had no cell phone service, and most businesses were closed for more than a week, including the Stock Exchange and the United Nations. The streets in downtown Manhattan were closed for emergency vehicles, so all of us who lived there felt cut off from the rest of the world. Rumors swirled on my block and among other residents in the building that another attack was imminent, that more planes were missing and unaccounted for, and that bombs had been placed all over the city, ready to be detonated. Everyone was terrified, and at night I couldn't sleep. I'd always felt relaxed and easy in my apartment, but now it felt lonely in my dark and empty room.

Living alone during a crisis—preparing for the storm, navigating your own or another's health problems or recovery—isn't easy. You might feel anger, resentment, or helplessness about having to do everything by yourself but let me tell you that you don't need to panic or wonder how you'll get through this situation, because you're truly *not* alone—you can rely on yourself. I remembered this one night a few weeks after 9/11 when I was sitting in my living room at two in the morning filled with fear and worry, and I closed my eyes, consciously inhaled and exhaled, and began counting my breaths. Although I wanted to get up and look out the window or call a friend, I stayed where I was. I put my hand on my belly and felt my respiration and said to myself, "I'm here for you," continuing for twenty minutes or so, until I felt more at ease and even a little tired. I practiced like this every night back then until the city came back to life and I felt less insecure and afraid.

> Pay particular attention to yourself right now. If you're seized with an overwhelming sense of aloneness—of feeling separate from everyone else—it's time to reach out as you can. Contact a friend or a mental health hotline like SAMHSA.[2]

You know you can rely on yourself because others already rely on you—you're a good friend, a caring parent, a loving pet mom or dad, and/or a helpful neighbor and colleague. When you're alone and scared, it's time to give yourself all that you share so easily and naturally with others. Treat your body, emotions, and thoughts as you would your dearest, closest loved one. Adopt an attitude toward yourself as you might toward a ten-year-old child coming home after school—one of interest and kindness and care. If you feel scared, sit still, wrap your arms across your chest, give yourself a hug, and say, "I can hear you, fear." If you're bored, rub your hands up and down your arms and count your breaths to ten and do mindful walking in your kitchen slowly.

Don't be afraid to reach out to others, but during a difficult time you might be even more isolated than usual, sheltering in a situation without electricity or unable to drive the few miles to your nearest neighbor or grocery store during a storm. If this happens, it's important that you pay consistent, loving attention to yourself. Monitor your habits to ensure you're not sleeping or eating too much or too little and that you're exercising regularly. Keep up with your personal hygiene and tidy your home regularly. Go outside if possible. Make it a habit to regularly turn off your devices and do something you enjoy—walk, take a bath, cook, or read a book.

> The Buddha encouraged his students to be "lamps unto themselves." His teachings enable anyone to discover protection, love, and rest within themselves. Buddhists know that our safest home is not external, because we can't control the world. Instead, our safest home is right here, right now, where we can be free from worry, neediness, or stupidity. So even if you're alone, you always have the ability to connect—*to come home*—to yourself. Direct your attention inward with mindfulness and compassion and experience your own friendship and kindness at any time, in any circumstance.

Practice 17: Being Here for You

Our lives are so filled with distraction and interaction, that sometimes we lose our most important connection—to ourselves. By coming back to this moment and touching your own experience, you'll discover your peaceful and compassionate home and feel less lonely, more whole, and at ease.

1. Shut off any devices, find a quiet seat, and close your eyes. Take five conscious breaths, paying attention to each inhale and exhale.

2. Put your hand on your belly and ask yourself, "How am I doing?"

3. Pay attention to your response.

4. You might hear yourself say, "I'm tired." Maybe your eyes are heavy or your back aches. Or maybe your favorite person comes to mind accompanied by a sense of longing.

5. Say to yourself, "It's okay. I'm here for you."

6. Whatever arises, just listen. You don't have to change your feelings or make anything happen. You're just experiencing you.

7. Remember, you don't have to fix or correct or improve anything that you're sensing or feeling. Just let yourself be a good listener and friend to yourself. Give and receive whatever reassurance or encouragement you might need.

8. Breathe and listen in stillness for a few minutes, then ask the question again and respond as instructed. You can repeat the question as many times as you like.

9. Do this for at least ten minutes. Try to practice it often when you're alone during an upsetting or scary time. You can also practice this exercise while you're in bed trying to sleep or lying awake in the night.

CHAPTER 18

Don't Lose Yourself

Feeling vulnerable, imperfect, and afraid is human. It's when we lose our capacity to hold space for these struggles that we become dangerous.

—BRENÉ BROWN[1]

AFTER THIRTY MINUTES OF EXPLAINING TO TWO DIFFERENT departments about my damaged car, I sat on hold for another twenty minutes. By the time the third representative got on the line and asked "How can I help you?" I lost my patience and blurted angrily, "How many times to I have to repeat my story?" Then I launched into a loud complaint about the insurance company, the service, and the accident. Hearing my shouts, my husband came into the room and said quietly, "Don't lose yourself."

"Don't lose yourself" is the phrase I say when I'm in a difficult situation and I'm not paying attention to my words or actions. If you're in a crisis right now, there might be times when you lose yourself too, and that is a signal for you to pause, take a breath, and begin again. When you're not paying attention, you're more likely to hurt someone with your words or actions or do something that is not going to help your situation at all.

If you notice that your mind is very busy or very sluggish—if you're jumping from one thing to the next or spacing out—you may have lost yourself. Stop and take a breath, raise your arms over your head, and say to yourself, "I'm here."

There are different ways to lose yourself—some of us get loud, angry, or critical, and others "zone out" and disconnect from what's going on entirely. Christopher played games on the Xbox in his man cave next to the utility room when he was stressed out. He didn't notice what was happening in the house or hear the kids when they called him, and his wife finally mentioned it during their couples therapy session. He realized he needed to learn to manage his stress differently so that he could connect with his family and himself.

In Buddhism, the main goal of practice is to notice and pay attention to whatever sensations and perceptions are arising in the present moment, both internally and externally. Because of the way our minds work—easily distracted by what we feel is pleasant or unpleasant—we have to keep bringing our attention back to our present moment experience over and over again. Our thoughts are constantly leading us away from the present and into plans for the future or memories of the past. That's why, in meditation, we're always beginning again and again. And it's the same for those moments when you lose yourself. You notice that you've lost touch with yourself and your surroundings, and you reconnect again.

If you've ever been hiking, you likely learned that the best thing to do when you're lost is to stop. Don't keep walking or you'll get even further off course and make things worse. Do the same when you've lost yourself. Stop. Stop talking, stop doing. If you're on the phone with the customer service agent, say "excuse me" and be silent for thirty seconds. If you're playing a video game, hit pause, and sit still and notice where you are. Take a few deep breaths and stretch. Remember that you can always find yourself, though you'll likely have to do it over and over and that's okay. You're always here for you, even if you don't know it.

Buddhists are supported in our efforts to develop our hearts and minds by "taking refuge" or "going for refuge." This means putting our faith in what is trustworthy and true—our own inherent worthiness, practices and teachings that lead to freedom, and wise friends who support our efforts. These three refuges are traditionally called the Buddha, the dharma, and the sangha (community). The act of taking refuge is especially beneficial if you're feeling lost, confused, or discouraged, and even if you're not Buddhist, you can always find refuge and safety in these supports. All you need to do is to put your hand on your heart and say to yourself, "I take refuge in my own wise and open nature; I take refuge in activities that lead me to recognize my own wise and open nature, and I take refuge with others who support me in finding my own wise and open nature."

Practice 18: Coming Home

This meditation is especially helpful if you're feeling disconnected from yourself. It's based on a traditional Buddhist contemplation used to develop a spacious, wise, and peaceful mind. By offering *metta* phrases to yourself and others, you'll feel supported and loved and know you're not the only one who struggles with self-acceptance or self-criticism. You can practice it any time, but I like to do it while lying in bed, just before I go to sleep.

1. Find a quiet spot where you won't be disturbed. Place your hands on your heart or your belly, and notice that you're breathing, notice that your heart is beating, and notice the sounds entering your ears.

2. Then silently repeat the following *metta* phrases to yourself: *May I accept myself just as I am. May I be at peace.*

3. After a few minutes, consider a dear and loving friend, teacher, or family member, and silently offer the same phrases to them: *May you accept yourself just as you are. May you be at peace.*

4. After a few minutes, consider both yourself and the same dear and loving friend, teacher, or family member, and silently offer the same phrases to both of you: *May we accept ourselves just as we are. May we be at peace.*

5. You can repeat as necessary and practice for as long as you like.

CHAPTER 19

Do No Harm

Preventing war is much better than protesting against the war.
Protesting the war is too late.

—THICH NHAT HANH[1]

I BEGAN STUDYING BUDDHISM NEARLY TWO DECADES AGO BECAUSE I wanted to help. I wanted to learn to do or say something to alleviate the suffering I saw in myself and the world. But I learned that wise action sometimes means using restraint and renunciation. Instead of doing something and helping, I also had to learn when to not do and what to not do. Andres learned that when he came home after six weeks in rehab. He was eager to show his wife and daughter that he wanted to help and was able to contribute to their family. Every night he asked them, "Can I do anything?" and he cooked and did the dishes, and he worked overtime at his job to show them that he cared and wanted to be there for them. But after a month or so, his wife said kindly, "Thank you for your support, but the best thing you can do for us is to continue to not drink or do drugs. That's the best gift you can give our family."

If you feel overwhelmed with anxiety or fear, don't do something—do nothing. This means sitting still and taking a few breaths and resisting the urge to speak or behave thoughtlessly. Instead, give attention to what you're thinking and feeling.

Actions include our words and behaviors and how they affect us and others. Discernment is the wisdom necessary to know which wise action to use in any situation. We can develop discernment through mindfulness and insight and then choose to act or to not act as is appropriate. Choosing to act means using our speech or actions beneficially. Choosing not to act means using restraint to not say or do something that could cause harm. If you're not used to using restraint, it might seem ineffectual to not do something, but it's actually a powerful tool. Restraint can help you to break repetitive habits that cause you or others harm, which is what Kate realized she was doing to her twenty-three-year-old daughter Mo. Whenever Mo wanted to do something that worried or scared Kate, she angrily yelled, pleaded, or insulted Mo. Of course, this upset Mo, and she didn't call her mother very often. So when Mo told Kate on the phone that she was going to attend the protests in support of Black Lives Matter in Chicago a few years ago, Kate could feel that she was about to yell. She'd seen the news. The police were making many arrests and treating peaceful activists with violence. Although she was proud that her daughter cared about justice, she didn't want her to get hurt. She started to raise her voice, accuse Mo of being stupid, and insist she stay away from the demonstration, but she stopped. She'd been working with her therapist to be less reactive and could see that it was harming her relationship with Mo, and she wanted to keep communication open in case Mo needed help. Although it was hard for her, Kate took a deep breath and calmly and sincerely told her daughter that she was proud of her and that she loved her. Kate was relieved when Mo let her know that she was safely back at her apartment that evening—and glad she'd chosen not to speak impulsively and unwisely.

Knowing when to do and when not to do can help you break your cycle of suffering too. Instead of continually reacting thoughtlessly in the same harmful way over and over again, you can use mindfulness to notice behaviors that are causing you or others distress and commit to stop doing them. It takes time and effort to change old habits and deeply conditioned behaviors, but you can do it, and you'll be glad you did. When you stop doing and instead prevent harm, you avoid bigger problems from occurring, and deter crises from escalating. In fact, if we collectively learned discernment and stopped acting harmfully, there would be far fewer problems in the world. So much of the tremendous suffering that humans endure is not inevitable and doesn't require us to do something—it requires us to not do something. In fact, many events we call "natural" disasters—hurricanes, floods, droughts, and more—would be avoided if we stopped creating the greenhouse gases that are causing climate change.

The Buddhist path of awakening includes training in ethics, and the foundation of ethical behavior is grounded in restraint and renunciation. The Five Precepts, also called the Five Lay Vows, are ethical commitments Buddhists make to avoid actions that cause harm. They are usually chanted every morning, as follows:

I undertake the training rule to abstain from taking life.

I undertake the training rule to abstain from taking what is not given.

I undertake the training rule to abstain from sexual misconduct.

I undertake the training rule to abstain from false and idle speech.

I undertake the training rule to abstain from activities and consumption that clouds the mind—liquors, wines, and other intoxicants, which are the basis for heedlessness.

Practice 19: Creating Safety

Underlying all our actions is intention. If we cultivate an intention to benefit and not harm, it guides our thoughts, words, and behaviors and grounds them in wisdom and compassion for ourselves and each other. The following practice is designed to enable you to recognize that everything you say and do—as well as everything you don't say and don't do—impacts yourself, your closest family and friends, your community, and the world.

1. Find a quiet place where you won't be disturbed and turn off all your devices. Sit or lie down and take time to adjust your body so you can get still.

2. Give yourself a moment to settle yourself, and notice what you're thinking about and how your body feels. You don't have to fix or change anything, just pay attention with kindness.

3. Notice your breathing and take five conscious breaths by inhaling fully and exhaling deeply.

4. Put your hand on your heart. Remember a time when you decided not to say something critical to a coworker, when you didn't drive after having a few drinks, or when you took a walk instead of yelling at your son for forgetting to take the garbage out again. Breathe and appreciate your wisdom and restraint.

5. Next, close your eyes and think of everyone you care about, including yourself, and silently say, "By my actions may we all be safe from inner and outer dangers."

6. Continue repeating this phrase, breathing fully and consciously, for ten minutes.

7. Conclude the practice by saying thank you to yourself.

CHAPTER 20

Navigating a Health Crisis

The right food, the right nutrients, the right balance of hormones, light, air, water, connection, sleep, movement, love, community, meaning, purpose. Those are the ingredients for healthy humans.
—Dr. Mark Hyman[1]

So many of us have received "the call"—someone letting you know that from this moment on, your life has irrevocably changed. The call might come from a doctor telling you that the tests revealed cancer, brain damage, a broken bone; from a police officer informing you that there's been an accident, the ambulance is headed to Memorial Hospital, and you need to get there right away; or from someone you love explaining that they're no longer in remission, they might need another surgery, and they don't know the outcome.

When you're navigating a health crisis, you're dealing with one of the most stressful of life's challenges, so it's especially important to be kind to yourself. Managing the healthcare system, supporting and communicating with your family and loved ones, worrying about finances, and spending hours, days, or even weeks in hospitals and other institutions is stressful, heartbreaking, and exhausting, and you need to be sure to take breaks, ask for help, and practice self-compassion often.

Rosemary learned this after her husband had a stroke. David, a seemingly healthy forty-four-year-old man, was playing basketball with his friends on a spring day in Prospect Park when he suddenly stopped and said to his brother, "I think I'm having a seizure." His brother, Martin, a former army medic, noticed that David's eye was drooping and asked him to touch his nose. When David brought his hand to his face, he missed and touched his cheek instead, and Martin said, "We're going to the hospital." On the way, he called Rosemary and she met him there, where the doctors discovered two small blood clots in David's brain. Because Martin got him to the emergency room so quickly, they were able to prevent the worst damage, but David still lost his ability to speak or move his right side. For the next ten months, Rosemary's entire life centered around David. She made sure doctors responded to his needs quickly and appropriately, and if they didn't, she wasn't afraid to get another opinion. She implemented a schedule for their grown daughters and other loved ones to visit so he didn't feel alone, and when it was time, she toured rehabilitation centers and interviewed staff to get him into the best facility for his needs. When David finally came home, she had a ramp installed at the back door so he could get in and out in his walker, and later on his crutches, as he slowly learned to walk again.

Rosemary was able to do all of this because she took care of herself and she made sure she didn't burn out. When the social worker at the hospital told her about a support group for caregivers, she joined the weekly meeting, met others in similar situations, and learned mindfulness meditation. She took daily walks to the little park by the river and drove to the gym for yoga class every Sunday. Most importantly, she was honest with David when it was hard for her, and he was honest with her when it was hard for him. This intimacy and shared vulnerability got them through this difficult time as a team, and each felt the other was still a partner, not a nurse or a burden.

If you're dealing with a health emergency, bring your attention to yourself even if you're not the patient. Make sure you're breathing—inhale fully and expand your belly, and exhale until your belly draws into your back. Do this briefly for a few minutes and repeat often.

Anyone who's been in a healthcare crisis can tell you that it's also an unpredictable time with many ups and downs. You might be panicked and freaked out one day, organized and in control the next, and sobbing the day after. Compounding the worry and stress can be the uncertainty about treatment, prognosis, and even whether someone will live. It's okay—there's no one way you should feel during this stressful time. Remember that keeping yourself steady and healthy is necessary for your well-being and for those you're caring for, so prioritize it. This can be as simple as taking deep, calming breaths, paying loving attention to your body, eating when you're hungry, and taking a walk when you need a break. It could mean deciding to leave your mom's house for the night to sleep in your own bed so you can get some rest and recharge.

If you're spending time in a hospital, it's a good opportunity to practice *metta*, loving-kindness, which will keep your own mind calm and prevent you from feeling alone. You can include all the patients and their families and friends at the hospital too, some enjoying a visit with a recovering patient, and others deep in grief with a loved one in serious condition or near death. You can recognize all the employees and the support that you're receiving from them—orderlies and janitors and receptionists, as well as nurses, doctors, and administrators—who are all doing their best to heal and cure everyone in their care. When you're waiting or sitting, simply say silently to everyone, "May we be free from suffering."

One of the traditional daily Buddhist chants includes the words, "I am sure to become ill; I cannot avoid illness." It's a reminder that everyone, including you, will experience sickness, disease, and/or injury. If you're surprised when it happens, this reveals how deeply you've been taught to deny and reject this poignant fact of your precious human life. Though you probably know how important it is to try to stay healthy and access the best healthcare and medical facilities available to you, you might not realize that it's also important—and wise—to accept that sickness can't be entirely avoided, and it's not a sign that you've done something wrong—it's just a simple fact of being human.

Practice 20: May All Be Healed

When someone you know and love is sick or injured, you might feel helpless and desperate, wishing they'd recover but feeling powerless to make it happen. You might beg a higher power to intervene or demand medical personnel to do more than they can. You might also recognize how strange and futile it is to hope or wish that only *your* loved one heals when so many people around the world are also suffering from illness, disease, and injury. This practice encourages you to consider and include everyone who is struggling and to share your compassion and love so that you feel less afraid and less alone during this crisis.

1. You can do this practice anywhere—at the bedside of a sick person, at the hospital, in a continuing care facility, or at home by yourself. You don't need to find a perfectly quiet spot, but you do need to stop talking, so find a seat where you can be uninterrupted for a few minutes. Close your eyes and put your hand on your belly and notice that you're breathing. Take a few deep inhalations and sigh out your exhalations.

2. Think of the sick person in your life. Imagine them during a time of happiness. Silently say to them, *May you be healthy and free from pain.* Repeat this sentence for a few minutes, as if you're giving a gift to them.

3. Keeping your connection with the sick person, connect with yourself too. Imagine you and the sick person together during a time of ease and say silently, *May we be healthy and free from pain.* Repeat silently for a few minutes.

4. Next include all the other people in the world who are also sick. You can start by remembering everyone in the facility you're in, or anyone else you've heard about who has a disease or injury. Say to all of you, silently and wholeheartedly, *May we be healthy and free from pain.*

5. Before you conclude this meditation, return your attention to your breathing, put your hand on your heart, say to yourself, "I'm here for you," and thank yourself for your caring and kindness.

CHAPTER 21

A Note on Thoughts and Prayers

Prayer begins where human capacity ends.
—Marian Anderson[1]

For the past decade or so, it seems like a popular response to "thoughts and prayers" offered during times of tragedy, disaster, or crisis is to derisively mock them. To some extent, this cynicism is understandable because thoughts and prayers are not a solution to a difficulty or problem, and offering only thoughts and prayers—without taking other actions—won't help to foster understanding or change the underlying conditions that cause suffering. Much of the scorn is appropriately directed at leaders and officials who offer thoughts and prayers without accepting responsibility for dangerous policies and unjust laws or who deny that problems could be prevented or ignore how each of our actions affect one another and the world.

But the truth is, thoughts and prayers are not all meaningless words uttered insincerely by hard-hearted people. On the contrary, prayer is a powerful tool used throughout human history and in all wisdom traditions to support beneficial speech and skillful behavior and to connect us to the suffering of others and ourselves. By offering caring thoughts to those in need and generating loving prayers for them, we develop compassion and wisdom in our own minds and hearts, which enables us to clarify and orient our intentions and align our speech and behavior with our deepest values.

If you're sincerely worried for someone (including yourself), you can say a simple and quick prayer to let yourself know that you're not entirely helpless and that your love and kindness matter. You can say something like, "I appreciate you; may you be well" or "I pray for you to recover easily."

Many years ago, I was at a Buddhist monastery in upstate New York, looking out the window at the sweeping view of the Hudson River and letting my mind wander when the old Tibetan Rinpoche (teacher) said that Western people don't know how to pray effectively. I almost laughed because at the time I was an atheist and a materialist, and I didn't think prayer had any effect at all. I thought praying was a foolish and futile attempt to control things we can't control by begging a divinity to help us. The Rinpoche explained it differently. He said that useful prayers are not requests for God, Buddha, or any supernatural power to intercede, but rather are commitments that *we* ourselves will intercede—in whatever way we can. He said that successful prayers are not selfish wishes, but vast hopes for the well-being of all living creatures, including ourselves. He taught us to pray with the understanding that our hopes will not be realized due to magic or God, but instead will happen when all of us create the conditions for them to exist. When we pray effectively, we understand that so much in life—including old age, sickness, and death—is not up to us, and we concentrate on using our words and behaviors to contribute to keeping all of us healthy, happy, and free from suffering for as long as we live.

The words *prayer* and *aspiration* are often used interchangeably in Buddhist traditions, because aspiration is as powerful as a prayer—it's a strong desire to achieve something that can bring happiness. In the *Puttamansa Sutta*, the Buddha explains that these aspirations are like necessary nutrients for our well-being and provide strong sustenance to fuel our actions and give us energy to benefit and not harm ourselves and others.

Practice 21: Effective Praying

Unlike conventional prayers, which appeal to an outside god or higher power to intercede on your behalf, to grant wishes, or to favor you because you're special, aspirational prayers are prayers to yourself. They are intentions that you set to accept responsibility to promote happiness for others and yourself, as well as vows you take to commit to using your actions to lessen the suffering of everyone. Practicing aspiration prayers effectively reminds you that we all share the same qualities of gods, saints, buddhas, and gurus—wisdom, compassion, and love—so there's no need to appeal to anyone greater than yourself, and you can be confident and encouraged in your efforts.

1. To practice aspiration prayers, create a small altar in your home. It can be a windowsill, a shelf, or a little space on your desk where you have pictures or photos of inspiring people or beings and perhaps objects that symbolize your connection with others and the earth, like shells, gifts, and figurines. You can display meaningful books or candles too. This altar doesn't have to be big or elaborate, just a space to honor what's important to you.

2. Sit near your altar quietly. Be sure to turn off your devices. If you like, you can set a timer on your phone for fifteen minutes, then be sure to set it out of your reach.

3. Put one hand on your belly and the other on your heart and bring your attention to the palms of your hands touching your body, noticing the rise and fall of your inhalations and exhalations.

4. Quietly say this prayer, "Through my good heart and wise deeds, may everyone be happy and free from suffering. May we all experience joy and peace." Repeat this silently to yourself.

5. You can imagine you're offering this phrase or other thoughts and prayers to strangers, people in your family, people you don't like, animals, the entire earth—all categories of living creatures. You can create your own personalized aspirations and blessings, such as "May we all be free" or "May we all be healthy" or "May we stop hurting each other"—whatever sentiment truly expresses your deepest wishes for everyone.

6. Before you end your practice, take a moment to appreciate your aspiration prayers and silently say "thank you" to yourself. You can take a look at the inspirational beings on your altar and silently say "thank you" to them too.

CHAPTER 22

Maybe You Need a Break

If you let go a little, you will have a little peace. If you let go a lot, you will have a lot of peace. If you let go completely, you will have complete peace.

—AJAHN CHAH[1]

DURING DIFFICULT TIMES, YOU MIGHT FEEL FEARFUL, ANXIOUS, tense, and worried. If you're like my cousin Kathleen's Aunt Mary, you'll try to keep yourself very busy by working, making Irish soda bread, calling the doctor's office often and politely insisting on more information, cleaning, writing, and indulging the cat. If you're like my colleague Larry, you'll do the opposite and zone out—surf the internet, play video games, watch television, sleep a lot. And if you're like me, you might read all the news and updates you can find and spend too much time on the internet, trying to get all the information to figure out and plan for what to do next—which usually gets me more upset. Then I wind up telling my husband how angry I am about the indifference and incompetence of whoever is in charge—the medical community, meteorologists, politicians—and the stupidity of the people on social media. At this point, he usually tells me to take a break and rest—and if I'm clear and wise enough to hear him, I do.

Move as often as you can! Use your mindfulness to pay attention as you walk up and down your hallway, to raise your hands and stretch with each deep breath, to wiggle your toes, to roll your head in circles, or to run around the block.

When you're caught up in a stressful situation, sometimes the last thing you want to do is to stop thinking about it—you are trying to figure it out, plan, or manage it. Often, the more you ruminate, the less clearly you can see the crisis and the more stress you give yourself and your body. Resting your mind gives you a fresh perspective from your problem so that you can approach it differently, and it builds resilience—your capacity to face difficulties without getting burned out or overwhelmed. Taking a break interrupts your habitual thought patterns by shifting the focus of your attention to something new, however briefly. That's why taking frequent rest breaks is important, even—or especially—during a crisis.

Rest is a state of present-moment awareness of your mental and physical experience. Rest is actively *not doing*—it's when the mind and body are still and relaxed, yet awake and alive. You might think of rest as whatever you're doing when you're not busy with work or obligations, but that's not true. Sitting on your couch watching a movie might be pleasurable, but it's not rest—your mind is still busy taking in sound, light, and story, making judgments, and figuring out plot and characters, and you might be eating, drinking, walking around, using your computer, or having a conversation with someone while it's on. With so much vying for your attention at the same time, it's impossible to let your mind and body truly settle down. Effective rest means that you bring your attention to just one place—the here and now.

Whatever you're facing right now, you likely have some painful and upsetting thoughts and emotions about it, and you might not want to take a break and feel them. You might prefer to have a drink, take medication to help you sleep, or keep your mind continually busy by making plans, calling friends, and working. There's nothing wrong with having a glass of wine to unwind, taking medication when you need it, or connecting with others, and I encourage you to do this, but if you're attempting to circumvent your stressful present moment experience, you'll create pain, fatigue, and unhappiness for yourself. When you let yourself take a break and rest in the here and now, you alleviate *dukkha*—the discomfort of struggling against your experience—and you can allow your life to unfold as it is right now without trying to improve it or control it.

I've written two different meditation practices for you to use when you take a break. Both will help you gather your focus and meet your restless mind with patience and kindness. You can do the "Time for Yourself" practice anywhere, anytime, and I hope you'll do it at least once a day. The "Mindful Walking" practice will help you discharge anxiety and lift your energy. Walking meditation has sustained me during very difficult moments—through the coronavirus pandemic when I was stuck in my home for months and after a long-term relationship ended and I couldn't sleep. Walking sustained my optometrist, Jesse, who remembered feeling restless and unsettled right after the earthquake in Los Angeles when he was a kid. Although his house wasn't damaged, the earthquake was a traumatic event nonetheless. His family had no water or electricity, and because of fires and downed power lines, it wasn't safe to go anywhere. His mom, a hiker who'd trekked in Nepal before she married, understood the power of movement, and a few times each day she held his hand while they walked from their front door to the end of the driveway and back twenty times. They didn't talk but they counted each step. It was so effective at calming his anxieties that he still walks slowly and counts his steps when he's feeling stressed out today.

Use your wisdom to decide which practice would be best for your break. If you're fidgety and anxious, do "Mindful Walking." If your mind is racing and you're feeling sad, try the "Time for Yourself" practice. Whichever you choose, you'll likely notice how much you want everything to be different when you let yourself get quiet. You'll also see that underneath your anger and upset is sadness, worry, or heartbreak. It's okay. Just keep breathing and let yourself feel it all. Your restless mind will grow calmer as you welcome what's arising with kindness and patience. When the practice ends and your break is over, you'll be better equipped to cope with whatever you're returning to, no matter how it turns out.

In the Buddhist tradition, walking is used as a contemplative exercise that not only provides physical benefits that calm the nervous system, but, as a form of meditation, trains the mind. Although most people think of Buddhists sitting cross-legged on a cushion on the floor, the Buddha taught four postures that are conducive to meditation: sitting, standing, lying down, and walking. All traditions have variations on walking meditation, and if you're able to go on a retreat—and I hope you do—it's likely your practice schedule will include periods of sitting followed by periods of walking. New students often think that the sitting part—when the body is motionless—is when the "real" training takes place, but that's not true. Moving or still, you're cultivating mindfulness and concentration so that no matter what you're doing—washing the dishes, driving to work, or taking a walk—you'll be able to keep your mind steady and calm.

Practice 22a: Time for Yourself

When you're in a situation that is stressful, threatening, or serious, you might feel like the last thing you should do is take a break. You might think you need to be continually taking care of others, planning, preparing, or just worrying, but without rest, you'll burn yourself out or get overwhelmed, and you'll be unable to make clear decisions or respond as effectively when needed. Taking time for yourself is for you and for everyone connected with you. Do the following practice as often as you can.

1. When you need a break (and even if you think you don't, you probably do), find somewhere you can be alone. It might be outside or in your car if your house or office is too busy. Set a timer for ten minutes and place it out of your reach.

2. Sit quietly, make yourself comfortable, and gently bring your attention to the rise and fall of your belly as you inhale and exhale.

3. Resist the urge to get up. Keep your attention on your breathing, gently feeling your abdomen rise and fall.

4. After a few minutes, put your hand on your heart and gently say, *May I open my heart to what's happening.*

5. After a few minutes more, think of a friend who is stressed and say, *May you open your heart to what's happening.*

6. Finally, include all of us in the world who are dealing with difficulties right now and say, *May everyone open our hearts to what's happening.*

7. When the alarm rings, take your time to shut it off and give yourself three deep breaths before resuming your activities.

Practice 22b: Mindful Walking

During the first few months of the 2020 pandemic, I felt depressed. I was stuck in my home and unable to see friends and family so I started walking a ten-block loop in my neighborhood every afternoon. Within a week, my mood brightened, I fell asleep more easily, and even my posture improved. Wherever you are during a crisis, disaster, or even just an upsetting time, I encourage you to take a walk. You can stroll around the hospital parking lot, in your garage, your front yard, in a nearby park, or on a beach. You don't need a lot of room or a special place to practice mindful walking—it can be done indoors or outdoors, in the corridor at work, on the sidewalk, or back and forth in your own kitchen.

Sometimes we're not paying attention to what's happening while we're walking—rather, we're more interested in where we're going or what we're doing next. Mindful walking means knowing that you're walking as you walk. Use the following instructions to guide you, and note that this practice can be modified for different abilities. If you're unable to walk, lift your arms up and down, blink your eyes open and closed, or take vigorous deep breaths. The purpose of the exercise isn't to walk—it's to use movement to help you connect with the sensations of your body.

1. Before you begin moving, stand still. Notice your feet feeling the floor or the ground holding you up. Take a few breaths and let yourself be still.

2. Take your first step slowly. Not super slowly but slower than your regular pace.

3. Resist the urge to listen to music or podcasts, and instead let yourself be present to all the sensations you encounter—what you see, hear, taste, smell, and feel, including the air on your skin.

4. Place your attention on the soles of your feet as they touch the ground. If you start to daydream or worry, just bring your attention back to the movement of your legs and your feet.

5. If you're outside, notice the sounds of all the other living creatures—birds chirping, children playing, car stereos, planes, bees, conversations. Remember that you're surrounded by life.

6. If you're indoors, notice the sounds of all the living creatures in the building. Your own breath and steps, anyone in your home, traffic from outside, people walking on the floor above you. Remember that you're surrounded by life.

7. Keep walking steadily and slowly for at least ten minutes. Before you end your session, stop for a moment and stand still. Thank yourself for your efforts.

Chapter 23

Be Joyful When You Can

You don't need to postpone being happy.
—Jack Kornfield[1]

As Hurricane Andrew approached Florida, Luna and Eamon were living on a sailboat docked in the Florida Keys. After they and the six other members of the crew prepared the vessel for the storm—taking down sails, stowing whatever they could under the deck, lashing down ropes and masts—there was nothing to do but wait for it to hit. Everyone in the small crew was an experienced sailor, and they took turns watching on deck, but the rest of the time they slept, played cards, told ghost stories, and ate junk food. They felt the storm the day before they saw it, the boat rocking and swaying despite only a light breeze, and when it struck in full force the next evening, the small boat banged against the harbor pilings. It was impossible to sleep and very scary. They knew it was possible that the boat could be damaged and take on water or even sink. But, amazingly, they had so much fun that night. They sat in the galley around a table that was affixed to the floor and rolled with the waves, sharing stories and memories of their sailing experiences, their families, and their dreams. Eamon taught them an old sea shanty that his grandfather taught him, and as they sang together, they felt happy, connected, and intimate. Luna knew the storm was damaging buildings, endangering people, and harming animals and marine life, yet here she was, alive and enjoying herself. She felt guilty and wondered if they should stop giggling and go to bed.

> If you haven't smiled in hours, sit down, close your eyes, take a few deep breaths, and smile—in appreciation for this moment, for your life, even for your sorrow.

When you're living through a potential disaster or someone has a serious illness, it might feel wrong to laugh or have pleasure. It might seem like you have to take each moment somberly, quietly, because you're in a situation that's not at all funny. But laughter and happiness aren't always thoughtless or superficial. They can also be expressions of wisdom—acknowledging the value and preciousness of life and the joy of being connected and together in a precarious situation. And they can express a poignant appreciation of what you truly value and love during a time of potential or anticipated loss.

After surgery, my dad was in a rehab center for a few months, where he wasn't treated well by the staff who didn't understand the needs of the elderly. I was on the phone with them daily, and we were worried about him most of the time, so my husband decided to arrange a special at-home date night together. We ordered food from a favorite local restaurant, danced to Instagram DJs, and later that night watched funny videos on YouTube. I showed him Charlie Chaplin being attacked by tiny monkeys in *The Circus*, and Lucy and Ethel working at the chocolate factory in *I Love Lucy*. He showed me the Marx Brothers singing "Oh Lydia," and Eddie Murphy skits from *Saturday Night Live* in the 1980s. We laughed and relaxed, and I felt less anxious than I'd been in weeks. But later when we went to sleep, I lay awake feeling guilty and ashamed. I thought, "My dad was really struggling while I was learning the Electric Slide in my living room. I *don't need to be happy—he does.*"

Buddhism says that we all need, deserve, and can be happy. You don't have to be self-sacrificing, have a special talent, or do good deeds to earn it, and you can enjoy the lovely moments that happen in your life while still caring about the suffering of others and the world. Happiness and the causes of happiness arise from wholesome mind-states—kindness, connection, caring, goodwill, love, and generosity, and denying yourself this happiness will not help anyone anywhere. In fact, if you're happy and you know it, it will help you recognize and appreciate all the blessings and positive circumstances you have, instead of taking them for granted. So go ahead and enjoy yourself when you can while keeping yourself grounded in the wisdom of change. Just as pain and suffering are impermanent, so too is happiness, and we can enjoy it while we have it and let it go when it naturally ends, as all things do.

In the Buddhist tradition, developing your capacity for joy includes delighting in the happiness of others. This is called *mudita*. It's our capacity to appreciate and celebrate the success, happiness, and good fortune of other people. The happy feeling that arises so easily in our hearts at a wedding, a graduation, or after a dear friend gets a promotion is *mudita*. During a crisis, practicing *mudita* can help us gladden our minds and not feel so down amid our own hard circumstances as we remember there are those right now enjoying a birthday, blessing a baby, getting news of a successful surgery, or celebrating any other reason for rejoicing and delight.

Practice 23: Sharing Delight

If a natural disaster is imminent, or you're in a moment of collective fear and worry, or someone you love is suffering, you might feel selfish or wrong to feel happy. But the ability to experience joy as well as sorrow is an expression of deep wisdom and appreciation for your life and for all life. Including moments of ease and connection is also a way to keep your mind balanced, so that you're not lost in terror and anxiety. Try this practice if you're struggling with allowing yourself to feel happiness right now.

1. The first step is to acknowledge that you're feeling ashamed, guilty, undeserving, or whatever it is you're feeling that is complicating your moment of happiness. So take a moment to listen to what's arising, to the thoughts or feelings that are telling you it's bad or wrong to feel good. Just stand still and listen.

2. Then sit or lie down somewhere quiet, and put your hand on your heart.

3. Take a few breaths through your nose (if you can), bringing air all the way to your belly, then exhale fully. Do this a few times, gently.

4. Now close your eyes and think of someone who is easy to love, perhaps a child or a pet, and imagine they're sitting right here with you.

5. Say this phrase silently to them: *May you be happy and filled with delight. May your joy never cease.* Repeat this silently, as though you're giving them a gift. Do this for a few minutes and then let go of the connection with this being.

6. Next, turn your attention to someone who is a familiar stranger to you, maybe somebody who works at your grocery store, or your mail carrier, or someone you know in your neighborhood. Give them the same phrase, saying silently to them for three to five minutes: *May you be happy and filled with delight. May your joy never cease.*

7. Let go of your connection with this familiar stranger and put your hand on your heart and connect with you—maybe imagine looking in the mirror or feeling your own presence as you repeat the phrase quietly for three to five minutes, as if you're giving yourself this same gift: *May I be happy and filled with delight. May my joy never cease.*

8. Finally, allow yourself to offer this wish to everyone. You could imagine our ecosystem Earth or just have a sense of your kind wishes radiating from your heart to all living creatures and say quietly for three to five minutes: *May everyone be happy and filled with delight. May our joy never cease.*

9. Before you conclude the meditation, take a few moments of quiet and stillness. Then thank yourself for your efforts. Repeat as necessary.

CHAPTER 24

Don't Be Afraid to Give

When we give cheerfully and accept gratefully, everyone is blessed.
—MAYA ANGELOU[1]

NOT EVERYONE IS EQUALLY AFFECTED BY A CRISIS, AND WE ALL KNOW it. During weather disasters like hurricanes, floods, and tornados, those in poverty usually have worse outcomes, are more likely to lose their homes, and have little savings to fall back on to support rebuilding, repair, or finding a new place to live. With a health crisis, many people are without insurance, struggle to find good care, and are often treated unfairly and improperly due to racism, lack of access to doctors and hospitals, and other inequities. The root cause of all these problems—greed, hatred, and delusion, the Three Poisons—exists in all of us, so it's up to all of us to use our wisdom, compassion, and generosity to alleviate the cause of suffering as we can, especially during a crisis.

The Buddha taught that the most important activity for regular people like you and me—who aren't monks or nuns—is to be generous—to give and share. Unlike other religions, no external god will punish you for the "sin" of greed—instead, Buddhists understand that when you grasp and clutch and want more than you need, you'll cause yourself suffering. Sharing is seen as an occasion to recognize what you have, and giving is an opportunity to learn to let go. So if you're someone who is experiencing a crisis, and you are healthy and safe, have a comfortable place to live, and are financially stable, this is your moment to give and share. If you're struggling to find work and make ends meet, this is also your moment to give—perhaps only to yourself and your family. Whatever your circumstances, remember you always have something to offer—emotionally, materially, or spiritually. Giving and sharing includes your money, time, attention, and prayers. It includes support through donations and contributions, and giving your beautiful qualities of love, joy, compassion, and wisdom with everyone you can.

> If you feel tight in your heart by the suggestion to give, and/or you feel you don't have anything to share, take a moment to think of something kind you said or did in the past week for yourself or another. It could be as small as texting your son and telling him you're proud of him. Rejoice and remember this as evidence of your inherent wisdom and generosity.

Being generous doesn't mean being stupid. Use your good sense and be careful to protect your material resources as needed in difficult circumstances, but if you feel you don't have the time to offer kindness and care to yourself or your family, you're wrong. During unsettling and upsetting times when there is a fear of loss or danger, you might feel particularly ungenerous and even greedy because you're scared you won't have enough. You might have plenty of money and still feel afraid of losing it. You might want to horde goods like water and toilet paper, even though it's not necessary. You might be so busy or stressed trying to handle a crisis that you refuse to take a break to relax alone or to be with friends and loved ones because you don't feel you have enough time. Or you could be struggling so much that you don't believe you have patience, love, or kindness to offer anyone, least of all yourself.

If you think you're depleted, empty, and have nothing to offer, consider practicing gratitude. Gratitude allows you to appreciate your life, however difficult it might be, and to recognize how much you always have to offer. Being grateful doesn't mean overlooking your problems or hardships, rather it provides a more balanced view of what's happening to you right now. It lets you know that you have both resources and deficits, sufferings and joys, difficulties and ease, which in turn will help you feel more generous, open, and giving to yourself and others.

After Gena's teenaged daughter Darlene survived a car accident with only a broken leg, Gena was relieved, but she still didn't want Darlene to spend time with her friend Sheila, who had been the driver of the car. Sheila was badly injured and required months of rehabilitation to learn to walk again. Gena believed that Darlene needed all her resources to heal and that she shouldn't give any time or care away to anyone else, especially the person who caused her injuries. But Gena changed her mind after Darlene came back from a visit with Sheila, smiling and happy. Darlene explained that seeing Sheila made her feel so grateful to be alive and so glad that she could give and support her friend.

Darlene and Gena learned that gratitude is a powerful tool that helps you see your greatest treasures are your love, joy, compassion, and wisdom and that giving them away only generates more. Practicing gratitude lets you discern if you can give financially and materially to those in need without harming yourself, or if you can share your time and patience with those closest to you without losing control of anything or becoming overwhelmed. It can also help you recognize how much you're struggling right now and that you need to focus your giving to yourself—taking a nap, meditating, having dinner at a friend's house—before you can offer anything to others, and that's okay too.

In Buddhism, *dana*—the practice of generosity—is a foundational discipline. It's one of the *paramis*—activities that lead to freedom from suffering, awaking to interdependence, and liberation from grasping and clinging. Skillful *dana* practice means giving some-thing freely without conditions and also giving something mean-ingful that has value to you. If you're very wealthy and you easily give money away without paying attention or caring about those who receive it, then you're not practicing *dana*. If you have lots of old books on your shelves that mean nothing to you and you give them to a school, you're not practicing *dana*. But if you give with an intention to ease suffering or create joy, then whatever it is you're offering, you're truly practicing *dana*—giving from your great brave heart of compassion and wisdom.

Practice 24: Gratitude

Gratitude is complicated. Sometimes it can seem like a chore, as though you shouldn't feel bad about difficulties in your life, or you should ignore problems and focus on the positive. But real gratitude holds all the negatives and hardships in equal measure with all the positives and kindnesses. It is much easier to feel gratitude than it might seem, especially when you're sad or worried. But all you need to do is pay attention, and you'll notice that although there may be many challenges right now, there are also things to appreciate. Try some of these easy practices if you feel self-pity or can see only what's hard and unpleasant in your life right now.

1. You can practice gratitude simply by telling someone you love what you appreciate about them. Try to do it regularly, perhaps every day at breakfast or via text before bed each night.

2. You can also generate gratitude by remembering the people who've supported, guided, loved, and encouraged you throughout your life. It might feel like you're all alone and nobody has been there for you but look a little closer. Maybe your parents weren't so great, but you had neighbors, teachers, aunts, friends. Right now, you may feel friendless, but someone is growing the food that you eat, and others communicate their support via social media or text.

3. Another way to generate appreciation is to regularly keep a gratitude list, noting three things that you're grateful for every morning. Make sure to list three *different* things each day. You'll start to notice so much that you're overlooking right now—a recent entry in my list read "Grateful for my coffee, rain, and being able to start again."

4. It's fun to share a gratitude list with a friend or group of friends, sending each other your three items every day via text or email. I've been on a gratitude text chat for more than six years with the same eight women, and reading their daily lists—thankful for birds, jokes, naps, children, living alone but not feeling alone—makes me smile every day.

CHAPTER 25

What's Next?

"What's the most frightened you've ever been?"

"I once fell down a well in Vermont. It was 25 feet down and the water was freezing, plus it was too deep to stand. I was down there for 45 minutes with nothing to hold on to but a pipe. Luckily my neighbor finally heard me screaming, because I'd guess I had about 15 minutes left."

"Wow. So did you reflect on your life at all down there?"

"No. I was trying to get out of the well."

—*HUMANS OF NEW YORK*[1]

NOW THAT THE CRISIS HAS ENDED AND YOU'RE OUT OF *YOUR* WELL, you have a choice. You can choose to reflect, understand, and even transform whatever difficulties you just went through. Or you can try to forget what happened and insist on getting back to normal. If you pick the second option—as many of us do—you'll quickly find that it's impossible to go back to the way things were, because everything has changed. The crisis you went through might have completely altered your lifestyle by disrupting your finances, your job, or your community. Or it may have changed your relationships—you've lost someone or something you love, and your family will never be the same. And—whether you know it yet or not—it definitely changed you.

It took eight months of treatment before Elijah realized this. After the oncologist said his prostate cancer was in remission, Elijah awkwardly hugged and thanked him and left the office in a daze. He knew he should call his wife and his dad and tell them the news, but he needed a moment alone so he went down the block to the Starbucks café and sat on a bench on the sidewalk with an iced mint tea. He'd been praying for this day for months and now that it was here, he felt relieved—but also a little lost. It was sunny and the birds were singing and it was early spring and cold. He knew that he was supposed to be excited about working with his brother Jayson again— they talked about it all the time—but now Elijah suddenly thought, "I can't go back to that." He remembered the hospital and the surgeries and nearly dying from pneumonia, and now that he had a clean bill of health, rehabbing and flipping houses while running his real estate business didn't seem all that important anymore. His family mattered, his church mattered, and his community mattered. But he'd changed. Just as chemo had ruined his taste for coffee, his health crisis had ruined his taste for striving and stress—and left him with a deeper appreciation for himself and a yearning to make his life meaningful.

> If your crisis has ended, you might not be sure how you feel right now. Take a deep breath and exhale deeply and loudly with a sigh. Do this three times. Then put your hand on your heart and say, "May I welcome the future I cannot see."

As Elijah realized, a moment of great change and upheaval can be an opportunity to create new possibilities, but only if you can stop trying to imagine your future solely in terms of the past. If you insist that you want your "old life" back, and you don't like your new identity as a heart attack survivor, storm victim, or widower, you'll become resentful, embittered, and entitled. But if you learn to let go of your *dukkha*—your resistance to the way things are right now, the way *you* are right now—you'll see just how much appreciation, kindness, and wisdom you've learned through the challenges you faced. Meeting your grief with patience and mindfulness—instead of hardening your heart against yourself—develops real courage, and this, your great brave heart, is what you need, what your family needs, and what the world needs.

This wasn't your first crisis, and I'm sad to say, it probably won't be your last. But that's not bad news. It's just a reminder that you won't be defeated or destroyed by the changes in life and that you truly can be steady, calm, and brave all the time. By continuing to practice the exercises in this book, using your mindfulness, and cultivating your great brave heart, you'll be prepared to meet danger or distress—again and again—with wisdom and courage.

Sometimes I feel like maybe I'm not good enough to truly become compassionate and wise, and I wonder if I should find another teacher or buy another self-help book. That's when I review the Five Perfections—also called the Five Certainties—from Tibetan Buddhism. They're inspiring guidance that I use to remember that I have everything I need to be steady, calm, and brave—right here and now—and you do too. I have them on the wall next to my desk and read them every day. I hope you will too.

The Five Perfections

1. *When is the perfect time to practice? The perfect time to practice is always right now.* Whether it's stormy or sunny, you're happy or bored, or your body is stiff or relaxed, right now is certainly the best time to practice. Because you have everything you need and because you don't know if you'll have time later.

---

2. *Where is the perfect place to practice? The perfect place to practice is wherever you are right now.* If you're standing in line at the supermarket, eating lunch at your desk, or driving your kids to school, you can practice mindful attention and compassionate listening to yourself and your surroundings.

3. *What is the perfect teaching? The perfect teaching is whatever is happening to you right now.* It might be a moment of quiet and peace as you're sitting on your couch watching YouTube, a hectic meeting with a potential client, or a frustrating call with your sister. You can use any experience as a lesson in *dukkha* and impermanence and as training in using your thoughts, speech, and actions with restraint and benefit.

4. *Who is the perfect teacher? The perfect teacher is whoever is with you right now.* Your nervous and undecided client, the woman doing your manicure, your dog. They're your teachers, and while you're with them, you can learn the wisdom of clear speech, compassion for their suffering, and joy for their successes if you pay attention. If you're alone, then *you're* the perfect teacher, and you can do the same.

5. *Who is the perfect student? The perfect student is you.* You might not believe that, because you probably think that the perfect student is so much more attentive, intelligent, devoted, or disciplined than you are. That's what I thought for a long time. But I've come to realize that of course I'm the perfect student—we all are—because I have the same beautiful qualities and buddha nature as everyone else—love, compassion, joy, and wisdom—and you do too.

Practice 25: Awakening to Change

Time moves so quickly and sometimes it's hard to see all the changes that happen. This practice is a very simple meditation that you can do anywhere. It's an invitation to simply be with yourself, in this moment, as you are, without trying to fix or figure out or change anything. I encourage you to practice it daily, and after each practice, notice what thoughts, images, or sensations arise. They'll be signs and signals of fresh intentions, insights, and changes that can guide you as you move through the joys and sorrows of your life.

1. Find a quiet place where you can sit quietly, comfortably, and uninterrupted for ten minutes. You might be in your kitchen, at your desk in your workplace, or even at a table in the back of Starbucks. Set a timer on your phone or watch.

2. Turn off your devices and take your time getting settled into your seat. You don't have to close your eyes. Instead, you can keep them open, looking down, resting your gaze without moving your eyes around.

3. Take a few conscious breaths, slowly inhaling and slowly exhaling, feeling your chest rise and fall. Don't do anything except pay attention to your sensations for the next few minutes. Stay as still as possible, be silent, and let yourself relax as if you're sitting with your dearest loved one. Resist the urge to get up and send a text or get some tea or clean the sink. If you feel irritated or sleepy, it's okay, just take another couple of deep breaths. If you notice you're planning what to do next or tomorrow, it's okay, just take another couple of deep breaths. If you're bored, it's okay, just take another couple of deep breaths.

4. Whatever arises, meet it, notice it, and let it go. If it's something you struggle with, like guilt or hurt feelings or knee pain or a headache, you can silently note it—say "guilt" or "pain" and then let it go and notice the next arising sensation. Remain like this until the alarm sounds.

5. Before you get up or resume your work, take a moment to appreciate your efforts. Say "thank you" to yourself silently or even audibly.

Appendix A

Mindfulness Meditation Instructions

MINDFULNESS MEDITATION IS A SIMPLE TECHNIQUE OF BEING PRESent with whatever is happening inside and outside of you during each moment. By bringing your attention to what's occurring right now, you'll be less consumed with worries about the future or regrets about the past. You'll be able to be with whatever is in your mind, body, and heart, whether you like it, dislike it, or find it dull, and to develop your capacity to react less out of habit and more from choice and good sense. Anyone can practice mindfulness. It doesn't require special equipment, it's not religious, and it can be done anywhere. I suggest practicing these instructions for fifteen minutes each day.

STEP 1: GET STILL
Sit, stand, or lie down somewhere that is relatively quiet where you won't be interrupted, comfortably keeping your hands still. Get as comfortable as possible, with a straight spine and breathing easily, in a chair or a cushion on the floor. Eyes can be open or closed.

STEP 2: SAY HELLO
Take a minute or two to ask yourself, "How *am* I right now?" A response may come in the form of words, images, and/or bodily sensations—simply notice what surfaces but try not to get too caught up in it. Allowing whatever is arising to emerge can help us approach our body and mind with compassion.

Step 3: Come to Your Senses

Bring your attention to your body, noticing your feet touching the ground, your seat, the palms of your hands, experiencing your shoulder blades, the back of your head, allowing sound to enter your ears.

Step 4: Find an Anchor

Choose an object of attention on which to focus. This is most commonly the breath, but you can use sounds or the feeling of your feet touching the floor. If using the breath, find one place in your body where you can feel your inhalations and exhalations: the tip of your nose, your abdomen, your chest. Experience the sensations and movement of your body breathing, and allow it to anchor you in the present moment.

It's very common to notice that attention stays with the breath or body for only a few cycles before it wanders away. If you notice your mind remembering or planning something, see if you can simply come back to *this one breath that you are breathing right at this moment.* Don't worry if you have to do this a hundred times in a single meditation session. Each time you bring yourself gently back to your breath, you are strengthening your concentration—the ability to direct your mind back to the present moment.

Step 5: Say Thank You

At the end of the meditation session, take a moment to appreciate and acknowledge the benefits of the practice you just did—not only for yourself, but for everyone you have contact with that day.

APPENDIX B

Metta Meditation Instructions

METTA MEDITATION IS A BUDDHIST PRACTICE DESIGNED TO HELP you cultivate concentration, wisdom, and compassion. *Metta* is a Pali (the language of the early Buddhist texts) word that translates to "friendship" or "loving-kindness" or "love." But the intention of offering *metta* is to develop your loving heart by connecting with other beings and recognizing their wish to be happy, their desire not to suffer, and their deep struggles. *Metta* meditation is traditionally offered to five beings in a progressive order from easiest to love to the hardest; the order is self, beloved benefactor, dear friend, familiar stranger, and someone you dislike. Note that you may experience love, happiness, sadness, annoyance, crabbiness, boredom, or any other feelings during this meditation. This is normal and you don't need to chase or create "positive" emotions. Any time you notice that you've lost the connection with the person or the phrases, gently return your attention to the practice and begin again.

Traditional *metta* phrases include:

May I/you/we be safe.

May I/you/we be happy.

May I/you/we be healthy.

May I/you/we live with ease.

Step 1: Find a comfortable place to sit on a chair or a cushion on the floor. Close your eyes or open them softly and stare at the floor. Bring your attention to the physical sensations of your body: notice sounds entering your ears, the feeling of your feet, the sensation of your breath as it rises and falls in your belly, light entering your eyelids. Pay attention to coolness, tension or tightness, warmth, pulsing, or even pain. You don't have to change anything or fix anything, just patiently notice what's arising.

Step 2: Bring your attention to anchor in the center of your chest at your heart. Allow a sense of yourself to arise. This could be an image of you as an adult or as a child; it may be a sense of your own presence in your heart. When you've made this connection to yourself, offer the phrases silently, as though you're giving yourself a gift: *May I be safe, may I be happy, may I be healthy, may I live with ease.* Continue to silently offer these phrases, and if you stray from the words, simply notice this, re-anchor to your sense of yourself, and start the phrases again.

Step 3: Move your attention away from this sense of yourself and the phrases and repeat steps 1 and 2 for each of the remaining four beings: beloved benefactor, dear friend, familiar stranger, and someone you dislike. At the end of the meditation, take a moment to offer *metta* to all beings.

Appendix C

Healing the World Meditation

In many traditional texts, the Buddha is described as a doctor who diagnoses human suffering, the causes of suffering, and prescribes a cure to end suffering. The cure is the collective practices of the Buddhist path—wisdom, meditation, and compassionate action.

With this meditation, you can share the same healing aspiration with all suffering beings, including yourself. You'll need at least thirty minutes for this practice, so try not to do it when you're in a hurry or when you'll be frequently interrupted. I like to do it on Sunday mornings before breakfast as a way to honor the morning and the new week.

Step 1: Practice mindfulness meditation for five minutes (refer to appendix A).

Step 2: Make an intention. Recognize what is motivating you to practice this meditation. Perhaps it's your wish for all to be physically healthy or for you and others to be free from mental struggles. If you wish, you can repeat this intention that I like to say silently to myself to begin this practice. It's from the great Indian teacher Shantideva: "May I be the doctor and the medicine and the nurse for all sick beings until everyone is healed."[1]

Step 3: Practice *metta* meditation for yourself only, for five minutes (refer to appendix B). Close your eyes and put your hand on your heart. You can use any or all of these *metta* phrases or others that resonate for you at this time, repeating them silently to yourself: "May

I be happy. May I be at ease. May I be at peace with the way things are. May I be free from physical suffering. May I be free from danger."

Step 4: Gently breathe. Rest your attention on the center of your chest and put your hand on your heart.

Step 5: Imagine the countless living beings near you and far away—in front of you, behind, to your right, to your left, above, and below. These are called the Six Directions.

Step 6: Offer your beautiful qualities of love, compassion, wisdom, and joy to radiate from your open heart in the Six Directions. You can do this by repeating *metta* phrases or by imagining light radiating from your heart or just by having a quiet sense of connecting with other living beings. You don't have to pick or choose a direction or who gets your beautiful qualities. Let them shine indiscriminately on everyone.

Alternatively, you can imagine radiating your qualities on particular groups, including more and more groups until you encompass all living beings. For example, you can offer love and wisdom to yourself and your family, then imagine including the people in your city, your state, your country, and the earth, and then including all the animals too. Or you can choose different categories of beings, such as all who are sleeping and all who are not sleeping or all beings with feathers, with skin, with scales, with fur.

Step 7: Let go of radiating your practice and bring your attention to your breath and body. Rest in silence for a few minutes.

Step 8. Thank yourself for your practice. Before getting up, stretch or move gently as feels useful to your body.

Brahmavihara *Paritta*[1]

Protection Chant of the Four Immeasurable Qualities

PARITTAS ARE SUTTAS—BUDDHIST TEACHINGS—THAT ARE RECITED to dispel difficulties, suffering, and misfortune. *Paritta* means protection, and chanting a *paritta* is a safeguard against afflictive thoughts and difficult emotions by filling our mind with wholesome aspirations and our ears with beautiful sound. I encourage you to read this *paritta*, translated from the Pali language, aloud, perhaps even singing it in a rhythmic chant. If you say it regularly, its beautiful aspirations will guide your intentions and protect you from mental suffering and the poisons of greed, hatred, and delusion.

Aham sukhito homi,	May I be happy,
Niddukkho homi,	May I be free from stress and pain,
Avero homi,	May I be free from animosity,
Abyapajjo homi,	May I be free from oppression,
Anigho homi,	May I be free from trouble,
Sukhi attanam pariharami,	May I look after myself with ease,
Sabbe satta sukhita hontu,	May all living beings be free from animosity,
Sabbe satta abyapajja hontu,	May all living beings be free from oppression,

Sabbe satta anigha hontu,	May all living beings be free from trouble,
Sabbe satta sukhi attanam pariharantu,	May all living beings look after themselves with ease,
Sabbe satta sabbadukkha pamuncantu,	May all living beings be free from all stress and suffering,
Sabbe satta laddhasampattito ma vigacchantu,	May all living beings not be deprived of the good fortune they have attained,
Sabbe satta kammassaka kammadayada kammayoni kammabandhu kammapatisarana,	All living beings are the owners of their *kamma* [karma], heir to their *kamma*, born of their *kamma*, related through their *kamma*, and live dependently on their *kamma*.
Yam kammam karissanti kalyamam va papakam va	Whatever they do, for good or for evil,
Tassa dayada bhavissanti,	To that will they fall heir,
Sabbe satta sada hontu,	May all beings live happily,
Avera sukhajivino,	always free from animosity.
Katam punnaphalam mayham,	May all share in the blessings,
Sabbe bhagi bhavantu te,	springing from the good I have done,
Hotu sabbam sumangalam,	May there be every good blessing,
Rakkhantu subbadevata,	May the *devas* [happy celestial beings, comparable to angels] protect you,
Sabbabuddhanubhavena,	by the power of all the Buddhas,
Sotthi hontu nirantaram,	May you forever be well,
Hotu sabbam sumangalam,	May there be every good blessing,
Rakkhantu sabbadevata,	May the *devas* protect you,
Sabbadhammanubhavena,	by the power of all the Dhamma,
Sotthi hontu nirantaram,	May you forever be well,
Hotu sabbam sumangalam	May there be every good blessing,
Rakkhantu sabbadevata,	May the *devas* protect you.
Sabbasanghanubhavena,	By the power of all Sangha,
Sotthi hontu nirantaram.	May you forever be well.

148

NOTES

EPIGRAPH

1. Thich Nhat Hanh, *Fear: Essential Wisdom for Getting through the Storm* (San Francisco: HarperOne, 2012), 87.

CHAPTER 1. HOW WILL I GET THROUGH THIS?

1. Lama Yeshe, *Becoming Your Own Therapist: An Introduction to the Buddhist Way of Thought* (Lincoln, MA: Lama Yeshe Wisdom Archive, 2003), 109.

CHAPTER 2. DON'T MAKE IT WORSE

1. Amy Schmidt, *Dipa Ma: The Life and Legacy of a Buddhist Master* (New York: BlueBridge, 2005), 132.

CHAPTER 3. LIVING WITH UNCERTAINTY

1. Access to Insight, trans. Thanissaro Bhikkhu, 1997, www.accesstoinsight.org/tipitaka /kn/dhp/dhp.24.than.html (accessed 8 March 2022).

CHAPTER 4. SUFFERING IS NOT A DIRTY WORD

1. Haruki Murakami, *What I Talk about When I Talk about Running* (Toronto: Knopf Canada, 2008), vii.
2. Thich Nhat Hanh, *Finding Our True Home: Living in the Pure Land Here and Now* (Berkeley, CA: Parallax Press, 2003), 109.

CHAPTER 5. HOPE AND TRUST

1. Merle Kodo Boyd, "Chiyono's No Water, No Moon," in *The Hidden Lamp: Stories from Twenty-Five Centuries of Awakened Women*, ed. Florence Caplow and Susan Moon (Somerville, MA: Wisdom Publications, 2013), 36.
2. *Saddha Sutta*, "Conviction," Aṅguttara Nikāya 5:38, trans. Thanissaro Bhikkhu, www .dhammatalks.org. Retrieved from www.dhammatalks.org/suttas/AN/AN5_38.html https://www.dhammatalks.org/suttas/AN/AN5_38.html.

CHAPTER 6. LOVE YOURSELF

1. bell hooks, *All about Love* (New York: Harper Perennial, 2000), 147.
2. Acharya Shantideva, *A Guide to the Bodhisattva's Way of Life*, trans. Stephen Batchelor, September 2, 2009, www.tibethouse.jp/about/buddhism/text/pdfs/Bodhisattvas _way_English.pdf (accessed 14 March 2022).

Chapter 7. Living with Grief and Loss
1. Sallie Jiko Tisdale, "Washing Out Emptiness," *Tricycle Magazine*, fall 2007.

Chapter 8. When Your Family Is Making You Crazy
1. Mary Karr, *The Liar's Club* (New York: Penguin, 2005), xvi.
2. *Akkosa Sutta*, "Insult," Saṁyutta Nikāya 7:2, trans. Thanissaro Bhikkhu, www.dhamma
talks.org/suttas/SN/SN7_2.html (accessed 8 March 2022).

Chapter 9. Watching a Crisis Unfold
1. "Bryan Stevenson: Finding the Courage for What's Redemptive," 3 December 2020, *On Being with Krista Tippett*, https://onbeing.org/programs/bryan-stevenson-finding-the-courage-for-whats-redemptive/ (accessed 15 March 2022).
2. Khenchen Thrangu Rinpoche, *Cultivating True Compassion: Bodhichitta and the Bodhisattva Vow* (Boulder, CO: Namo Buddha Publications, 2014), 97–99.

Chapter 10. Just Relax
1. Ryōkan and Mary Lou Kownacki, *Between Two Souls: Conversations with Ryōkan* (Grand Rapids, MI: William B. Eerdmans, 2004), 44.

Chapter 11. When You Need Help
1. Charlie Mackesy, *The Boy, the Mole, the Fox and the Horse* (New York: HarperCollins, 2019), 65.
2. "At Sedaka," Saṁyutta Nikāya 47.19, trans. Bhikkhu Sujato, *Sutta Central*, https://suttacentral.net/sn47.19/en/sujato (accessed 16 March 2022).

Chapter 12. When You're Mad at the World
1. Bayo Akomolafe, "Let Us Slow Down: Acting in Turbulent Times," *Báyò Akómoláfé* (blog), 9 November 2018, www.bayoakomolafe.net/post/let-us-slow-down-acting-in-turbulent-times (accessed 16 March 2022).
2. "*Karaniya Metta Sutta*: The Hymn of Universal Love," *Sutta Nipata* 1.8, trans. Acharya Buddharakkhita, Access to Insight (BCBS edition), 29 August 2012, www.accesstoinsight.org/tipitaka/kn/snp/snp.1.08.budd.html (accessed 16 March 2022).

Chapter 13. What to Do When You're Afraid
1. Tsoknyi Rinpoche, *Fearless Simplicity: The Dzogchen Way of Living Freely in a Complex World* (Hong Kong: Rangjung Yeshe, 2003), 255.

Chapter 14. When Others Behave Badly
1. Anne Lamott, *Almost Everything: Notes on Hope* (New York: Riverhead, 2018), 60.

Chapter 15. When You're Restless and Bored
1. Joseph Goldstein, *Insight Meditation: A Psychology of Freedom* (Boulder, NY: Shambhala, 2003), 80.

Chapter 16. A Crisis of Faith

1. Nyoshul Khen Rinpoche, *Natural Great Perfection: Dzogchen Teachings and Vajra Songs* (Boulder, CO: Snow Lion, 2009), 143.

2. See the work of Dr. Richard J. Davidson and the Center for Healthy Minds for more information about inherent empathy and compassion.

Chapter 17. Living Alone in a Crisis

1. "Stephen Batchelor: Finding Ease in Aloneness," 23 April 2020, *On Being with Krista Tippett*, https://onbeing.org/programs/stephen-batchelor-finding-ease-in-aloneness/ (accessed 16 March 2022).

2. The Substance Abuse and Mental Health Services Administration offers free resources, including a twenty-four-hour crisis hotline: www.samhsa.gov.

Chapter 18. Don't Lose Yourself

1. "Brené Brown: Strong Back, Soft Front, Wild Heart," 18 February 2018, *On Being with Krista Tippett*, https://onbeing.org/programs/brene-brown-strong-back-soft-front-wild-heart/ (accessed 16 March 2022).

Chapter 19. Do No Harm

1. Thich Nhat Hanh, *Being Peace* (Berkeley: Parallax Press, 2020), 98.

Chapter 20. Navigating a Health Crisis

1. "Mark Hyman, James Gordon, and Penny George: The Evolution of Medicine," 3 December 2015, *On Being with Krista Tippett*, https://onbeing.org/programs/mark-hyman-james-gordon-penny-george-the-evolution-of-medicine/ (accessed 16 March 2022).

Chapter 21. A Note on Thoughts and Prayers

1. Marian Anderson, *My Lord, What a Morning* (Urbana: University of Illinois Press, 2002), 255.

Chapter 22. Maybe You Need a Break

1. Ajahn Chah: Reflections, www.dhammatalks.net/Books/Ajahn_Chah_No_Ajahn_Chah.htm (accessed 16 March 2022).

Chapter 23. Be Joyful When You Can

1. Jack Kornfield, *No Time Like the Present: Finding Freedom, Love, and Joy Right Where You Are* (New York: Atria, 2018), 1.

Chapter 24. Don't Be Afraid to Give

1. Maya Angelou, *Wouldn't Take Nothing for My Journey Now* (New York: Random House), 81.

Chapter 25. What's Next?

1. *Humans of New York*, www.humansofnewyork.com/post/67594733526/whats-the-most-frightened-youve-ever-been-i/amp (accessed 10 March 2022).

Appendix C. Healing the World Meditation
1. Shantideva, *A Guide to the Bodhisattva's Way of Life*, trans. Ken Holmes, Katia Holmes, and Thomas Doctor (Dharamshala, India: Library of Tibetan Works and Archives, 2016), 40.

Appendix D. Brahmavihara *Paritta*: Protection Chant of the Four Immeasurable Qualities
1. Buddha Haksa Temple, *Pali Chanting: Pali Passages with English Translations* (2017), 153, http://buddhahaksa.com/uploads/1/0/5/3/105396541/completed_chanting_book_1st_edition_bht.compressed.pdf (accessed 10 March 2022).

About the Author

Kimberly Brown is a meditation teacher, author, and speaker whose work explores the transformative power and wisdom of love. A Buddhist student for many years, she guides individuals to create meaningful relationships through self-compassion, leads groups to develop connection and cooperation through *metta* (loving-kindness) meditation, regularly teaches classes and retreats at meditation centers online and in person, and mentors and trains new mindfulness teachers.

Raised in the Midwest, Kimberly received a BS from Hunter College in physics and an MA from City College in English. She trained for several years as a psychoanalytic psychotherapist and is a certified mindfulness instructor. She is the author of *Navigating Grief and Loss: 25 Buddhist Practices to Keep Your Heart Open to Yourself and Others* and a regular contributor to *Tricycle: The Buddhist Review* and other publications. Kimberly lives in New York City with her family. You can learn more about her work at www.meditationwithheart.com.